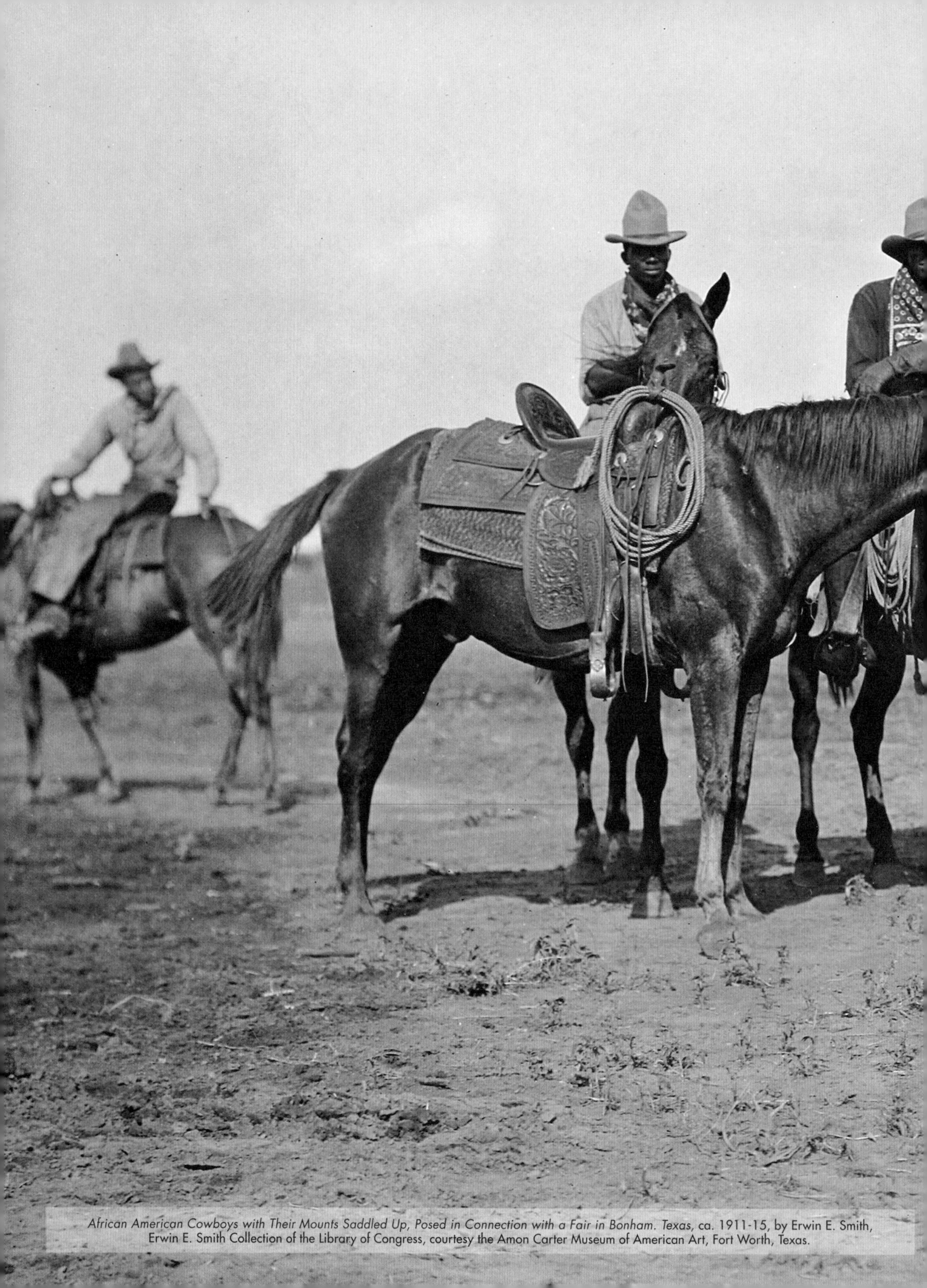

African American Cowboys with Their Mounts Saddled Up, Posed in Connection with a Fair in Bonham. Texas, ca. 1911-15, by Erwin E. Smith, Erwin E. Smith Collection of the Library of Congress, courtesy the Amon Carter Museum of American Art, Fort Worth, Texas.

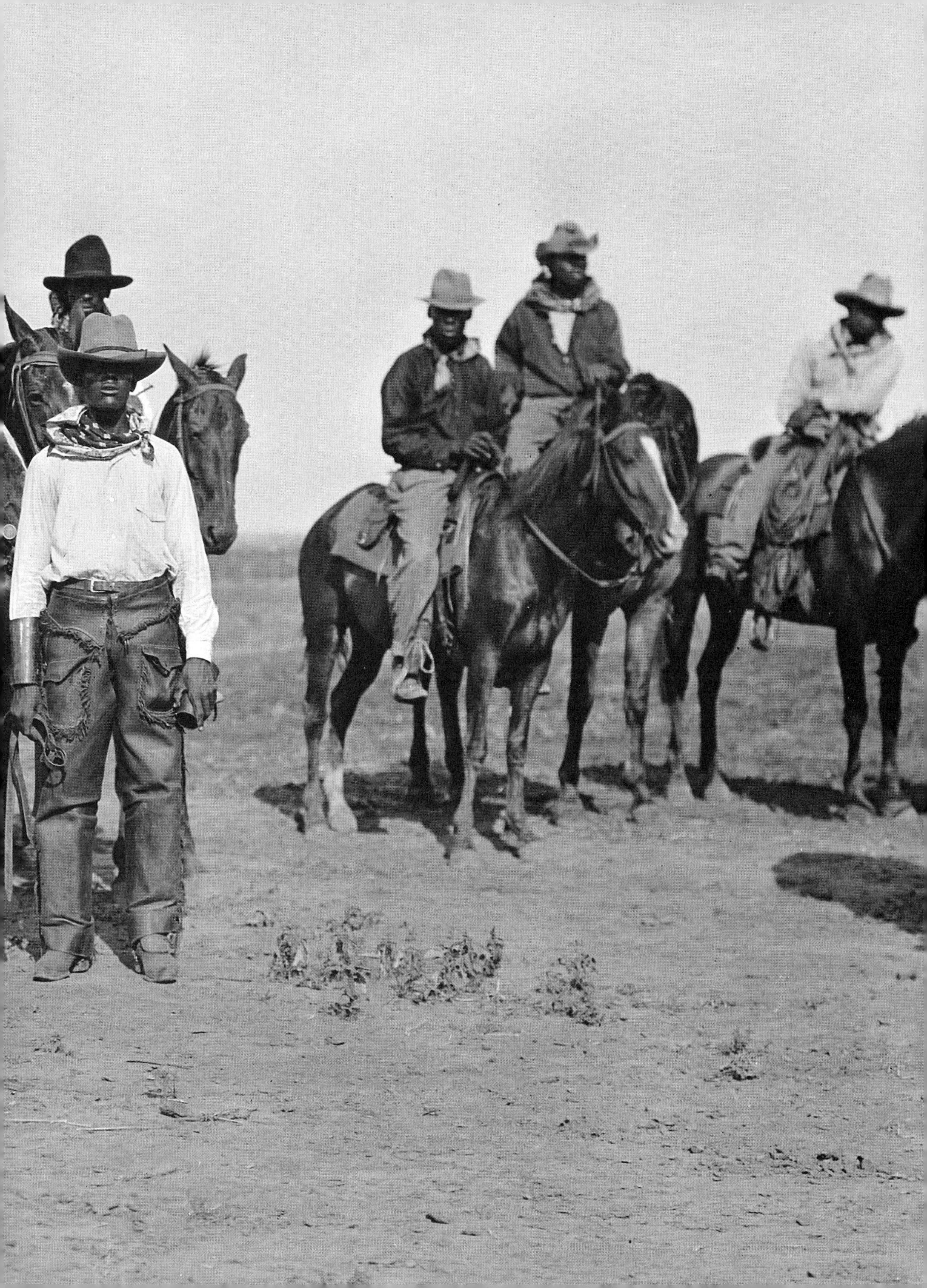

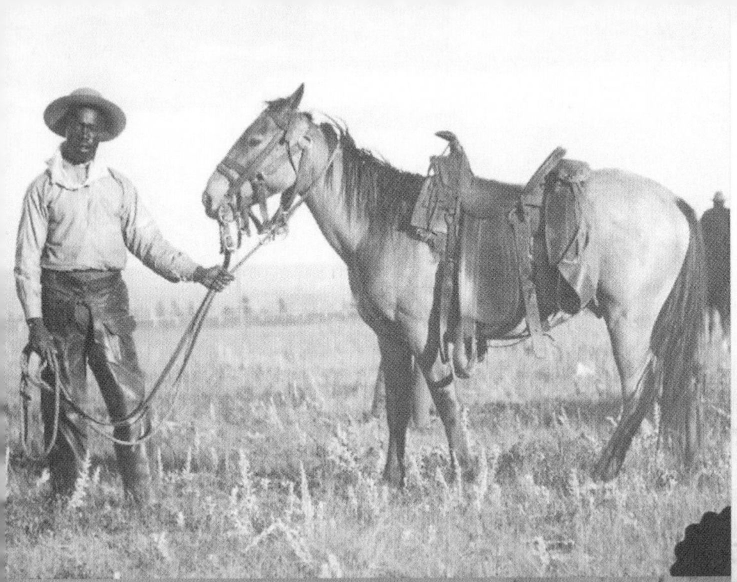
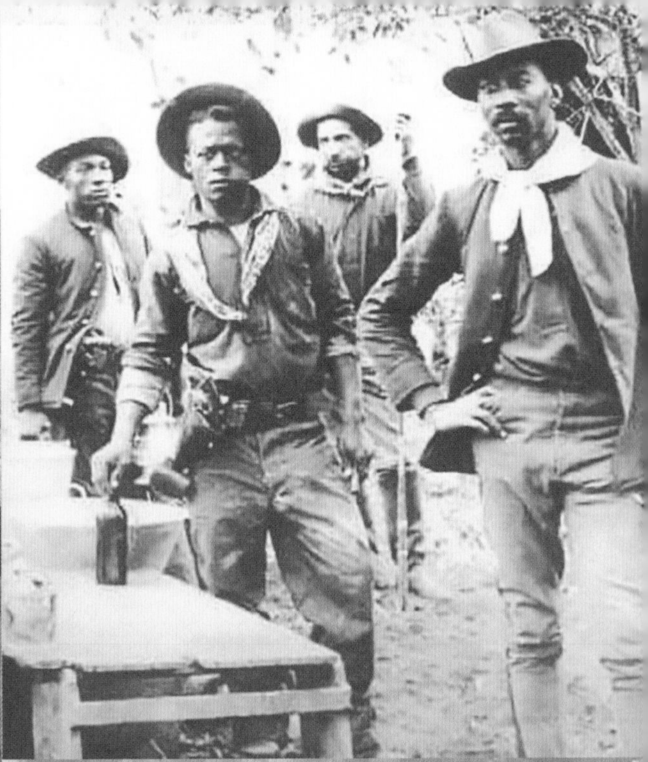
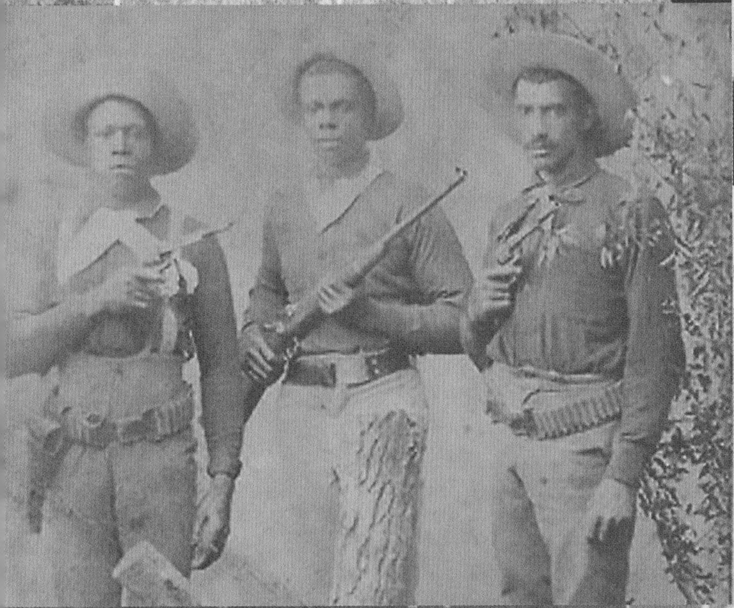
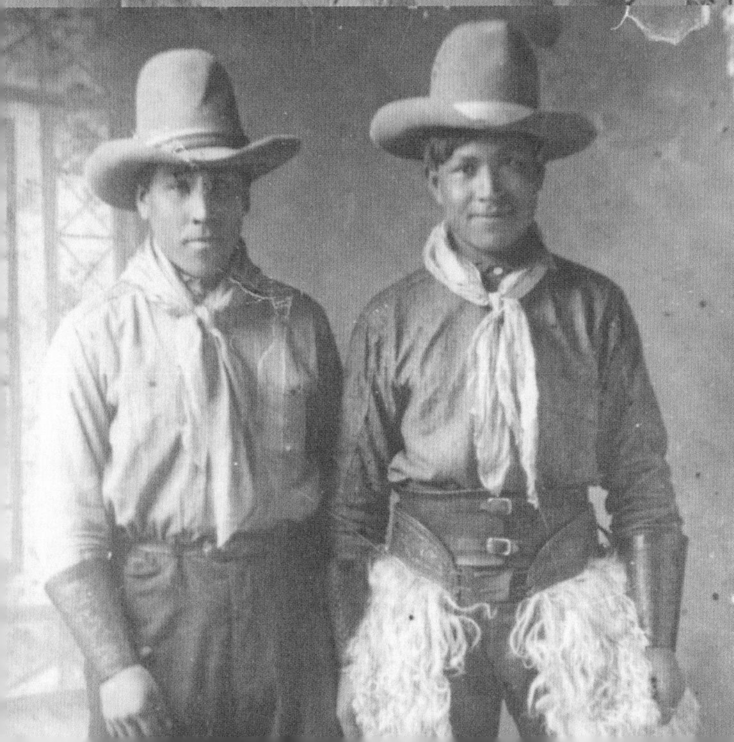
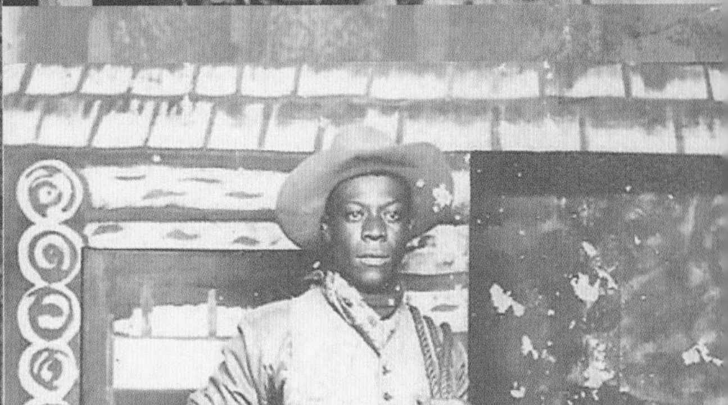
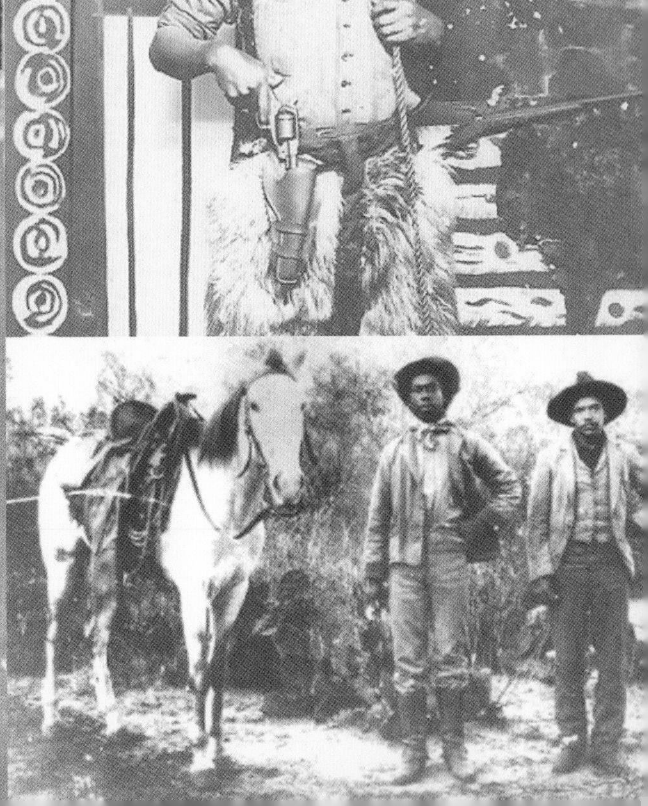

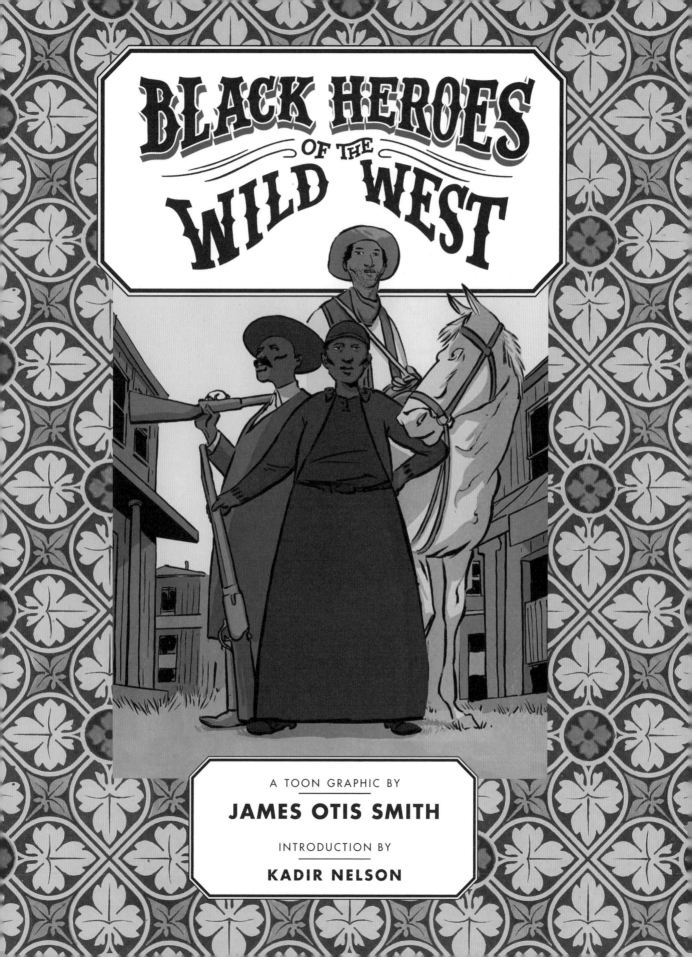

FOR A NEW AMERICAN HISTORY

Introduction by Kadir Nelson

The Gilcrease Museum, Tulsa, Oklahoma

In his 1889 painting, A Dash for the Timber, *renowned painter of the West Frederic S. Remington shows cowboys as a group of white men. In fact, a large number were Mexican or Native American, and as many as one-third were African American.*

Photography outside the studio wasn't widespread in the 19th century, so much of the pictorial record of the cowboys' lives was provided by artists such as Remington. During the 1880s, Remington traveled through the Dakotas, Montana, Texas, and the Arizona Territory to record the vanishing wilderness in sculpture, paintings, and drawings.

"Bronco busters saddling," wood engraving

WHEN I WAS FIFTEEN, my mother took me to the Los Angeles Coliseum to see Nelson Mandela speak. When he appeared, the crowd cheered for what felt like an eternity. They wouldn't stop—everyone was so excited, so jubilant. It made me want to paint images of the people who inspired me: Nelson Mandela, of course, Martin Luther King, Malcolm X, and so many more. I hadn't especially liked history in school because it seemed to be all about memorization. But when I realized that history is a string of stories—I was hooked.

I was introduced to the history of African Americans in the Old West as an art student at Pratt Institute in the early 1990s. At the time, I was working on a series of paintings that celebrated African Americans who had settled west of the Mississippi River during and after the American Civil War. As I delved into my research, I pored over the sparse documentation chronicling the lives of black pioneers, cowboys, and homesteaders on the Great Plains, and I was excited to discover enthralling figures like Bill Pickett, Nat Love, and Mary Fields. Before then, most of my knowledge of the Old West had been limited to books, movies, and paintings that featured cowboys and homesteaders of a much lighter hue.

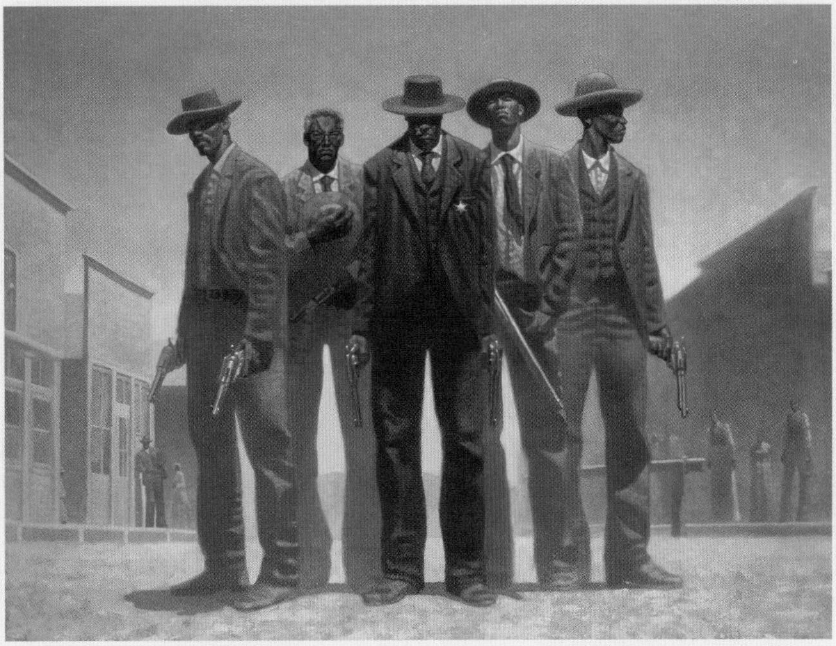

Courtesy Kadir Nelson Studio

Not all picture-making needs to be reportorial and historically accurate. Art can also be a legitimate way for artists to portray what they'd like to see and to let their imagination run free. Above, in an image called High Noon, *Kadir Nelson depicts a group of black men as the central figures of a typical showdown in the Wild West.*

As I conducted research for my picture book, *Heart and Soul: The Story of America and African Americans*, which was also partly set during this time period, I was surprised to learn that in some areas of the Old West, up to a third of the settler population was African American. This is why I'm so pleased to see a volume that celebrates this very fact. *Black Heroes of the Wild West* is a brilliant and entertaining offering from James Otis Smith. Through sharp and evocative storytelling in the exciting medium of comics, lesser-known African American historical figures will be introduced to new generations of readers. Smith's humor and wit shine throughout, and his masterful graphic design works hand in hand with the storytelling: the panel sequences are sometimes silent, while at other times they progress through dialogue or captions. Fascinating people like Mary Fields, Bass Reeves, and Bob Lemmons are given new life, and the endnotes are full of informative facts and images that testify to the essential role of African Americans, Native Americans, and Hispanic *vaqueros* in the Old West. Smith's début offers an extraordinary introduction into this facet of America's rich history. It's time that we hear every American's story: from every background and creed, we've all worked together to weave the grand tapestry of America.

Red, White, and Weary Blues, *is one of Nelson's illustrations for* The Undefeated, *written by Kwame Alexander. The authors wanted to honor the spirit of the nearly 200,000 newly liberated men who joined the Union Army after the 1863 Emancipation Proclamation.*

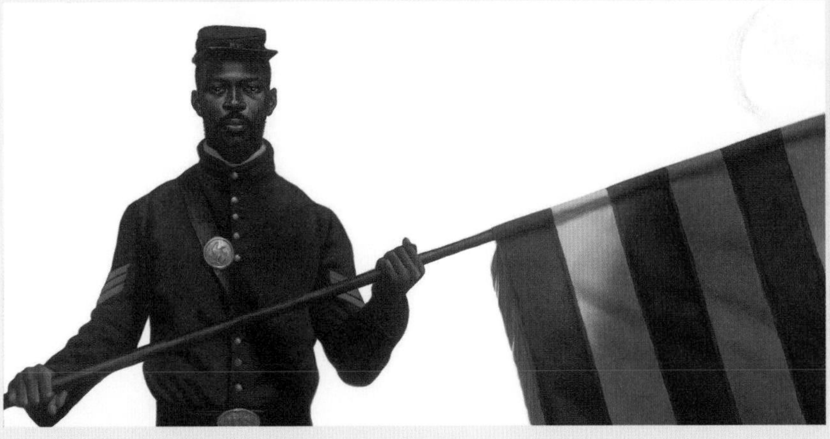

From THE UNDEFEATED by Kwame Alexander, illustrated by Kadir Nelson.
Reprinted by permission of Houghton Mifflin Harcourt Publishing Company.

TOP 10 BOOKS FOR KIDS —*NEW YORK PUBLIC LIBRARY*
FAVORITE BOOKS OF 2020 —*NPR BOOK CONCIERGE*
LITTLE MAVERICK GRAPHIC NOVEL READING LIST —*TEXAS LIBRARY ASSOCIATION*
A JUNIOR LIBRARY GUILD GOLD STANDARD SELECTION

For Yvonne

Editorial Director & Book Design: FRANÇOISE MOULY

Guest Editor: SAMUEL RUTTER

Research & Supplementary Material: FRANÇOISE MOULY

Colors: FRANK REYNOSO

Title lettering: PAUL LESSER

JAMES OTIS SMITH'S artwork was drawn in pen and ink on bristol board
and then colored digitally by Frank Reynoso.

FOR VISUAL READERS
TOON
GRAPHICS

A TOON Graphic™ © 2020 James Otis Smith & TOON Books, an imprint of Astra Books for Young Readers, a division of Astra Publishing House. Introduction and images on page 7 © Kadir Nelson. Erwin E. Smith photo on page 2 © Erwin E. Smith Foundation. All historical material © individual rights owners. Copying or digitizing this book for storage, display, or distribution in any other medium is strictly prohibited. All rights reserved. For information about permission to reproduce selections from this book, please contact permissions@astrapublishinghouse.com. TOON Graphics™, TOON Books®, LITTLE LIT® and TOON Into Reading!™ are trademarks of Astra Publishing House. All our books are Smyth Sewn (the highest library-quality binding available) and printed with soy-based inks on acid-free, woodfree paper harvested from responsible sources. Printed in China. Library of Congress Cataloging-in-Publication Data: Names: Smith, James Otis, author, illustrator. | Mouly, Françoise, editor.| Nelson, Kadir, writer of introduction. Title: Black heroes of the wild west / a Toon Graphic by James Otis Smith, introduction by Kadir Nelson. Includes bibliographical references. | Audience: Grades 4-6 | Summary: ""Black Heroes of the Wild West" celebrates the extraordinary true tales of three Black historical figures in the Old West: Mary "Stagecoach" Fields, a cardplaying coach driver; Bass Reeves, the first Black Deputy US Marshall west of the Mississippi; and Bob Lemmons, a cowboy famous for his ability to tame mustangs"-- Provided by publisher. Subjects: LCSH: Fields, Mary, approximately 1832-1914--Juvenile literature.| Reeves, Bass--Juvenile literature. | Lemmons, Bob--Juvenile literature. | African American pioneers--Juvenile literature. | African American cowboys--Juvenile literature. | African Americans--History--Juvenile literature. | LCGFT: Graphic novels. Classification: LCC E185.925 .S65 2020 | DDC 978.7800496073--dc23 LC record available at https://lccn.loc.gov/2020017599

ISBN: 978-1-943145-51-5 (hardcover)   978-1-943145-52-2 (paperback)

22 23 24 25 26 C&C 10 9 8 7 6 5 4 3

WWW.TOON-BOOKS.COM

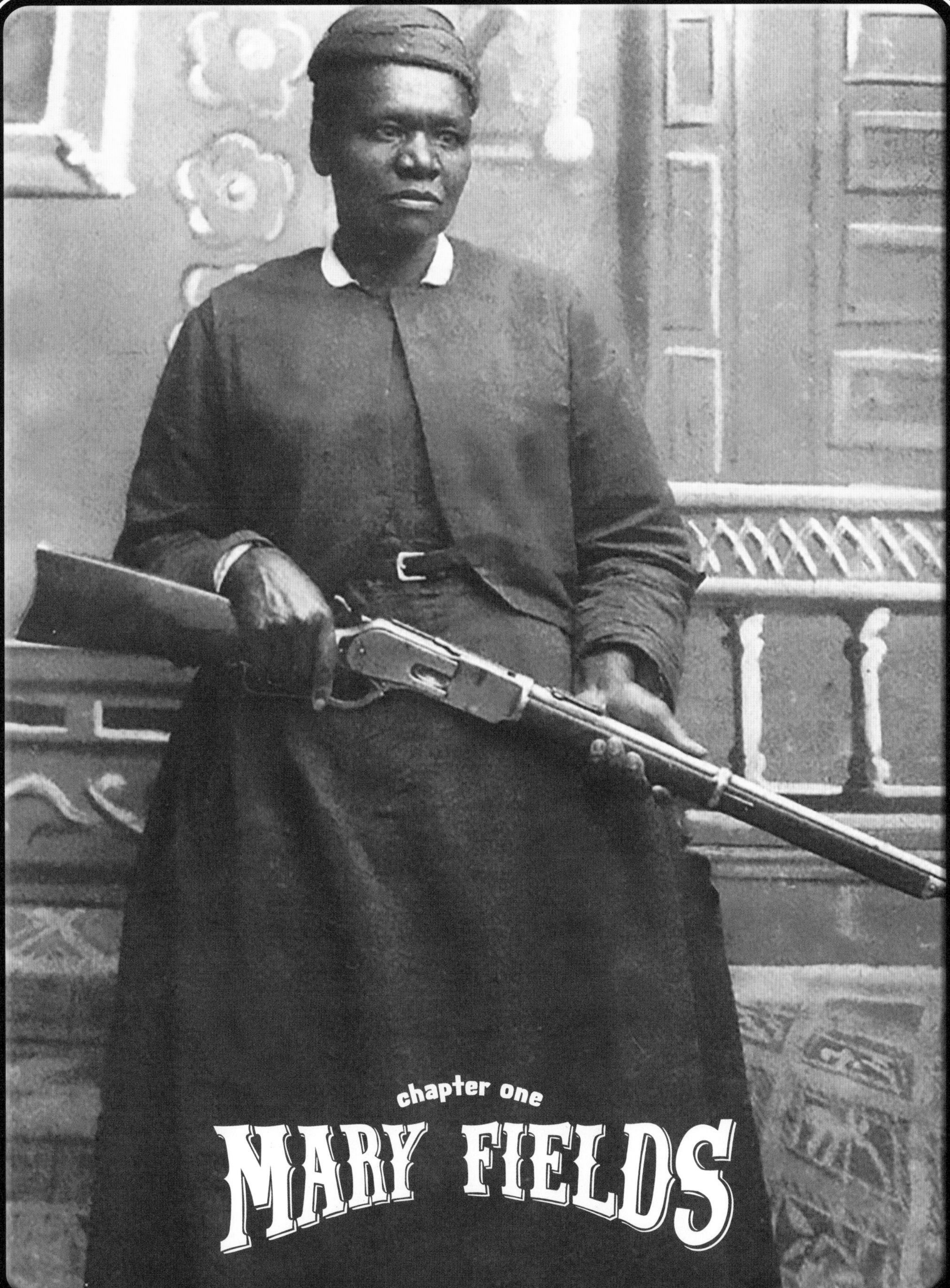

chapter one

MARY FIELDS

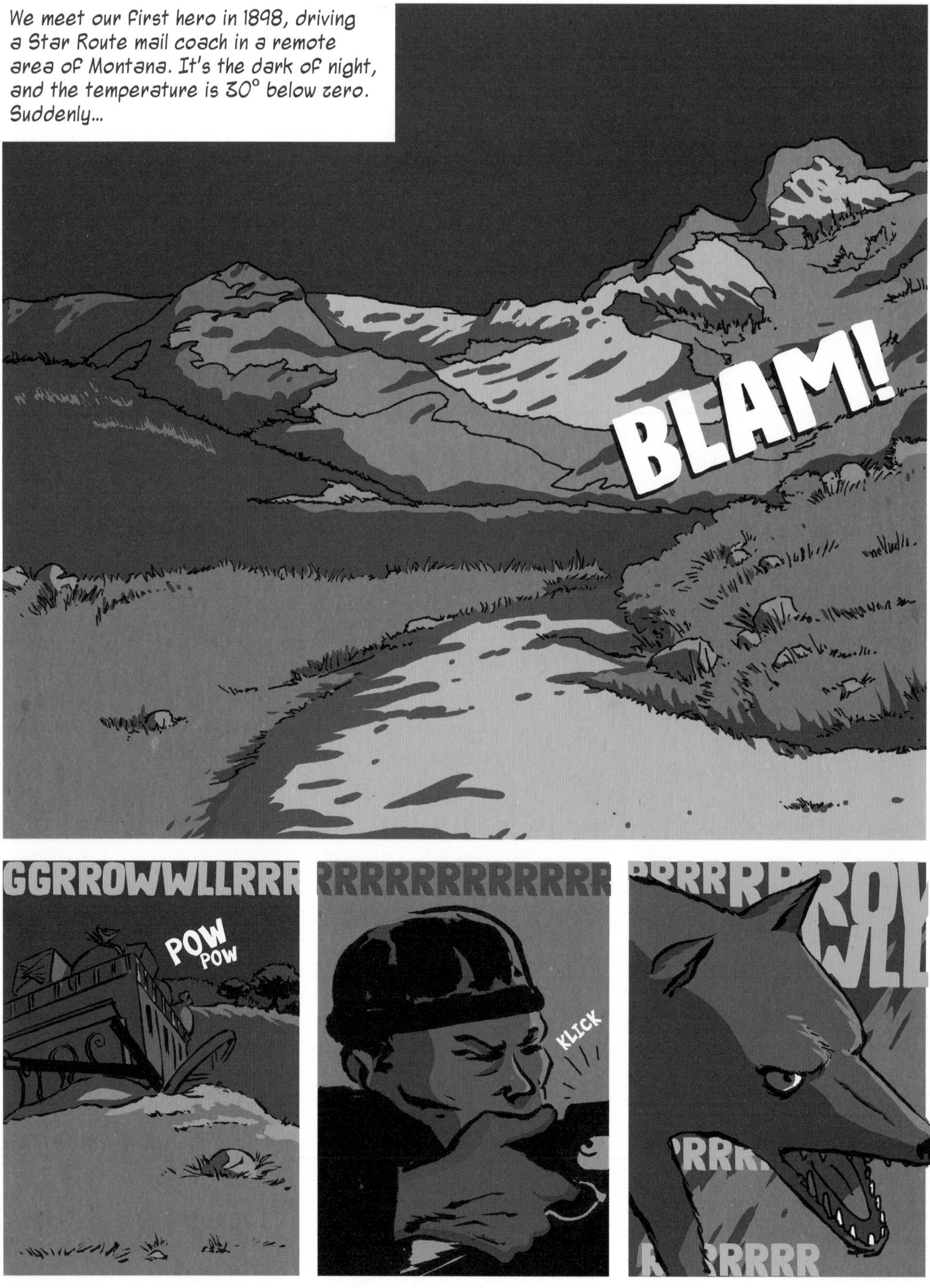
We meet our first hero in 1898, driving a Star Route mail coach in a remote area of Montana. It's the dark of night, and the temperature is 30° below zero. Suddenly...
BLAM!
GGRROWWLLRRR
POW
POW
RRRRRRRRRRRRR
KLICK

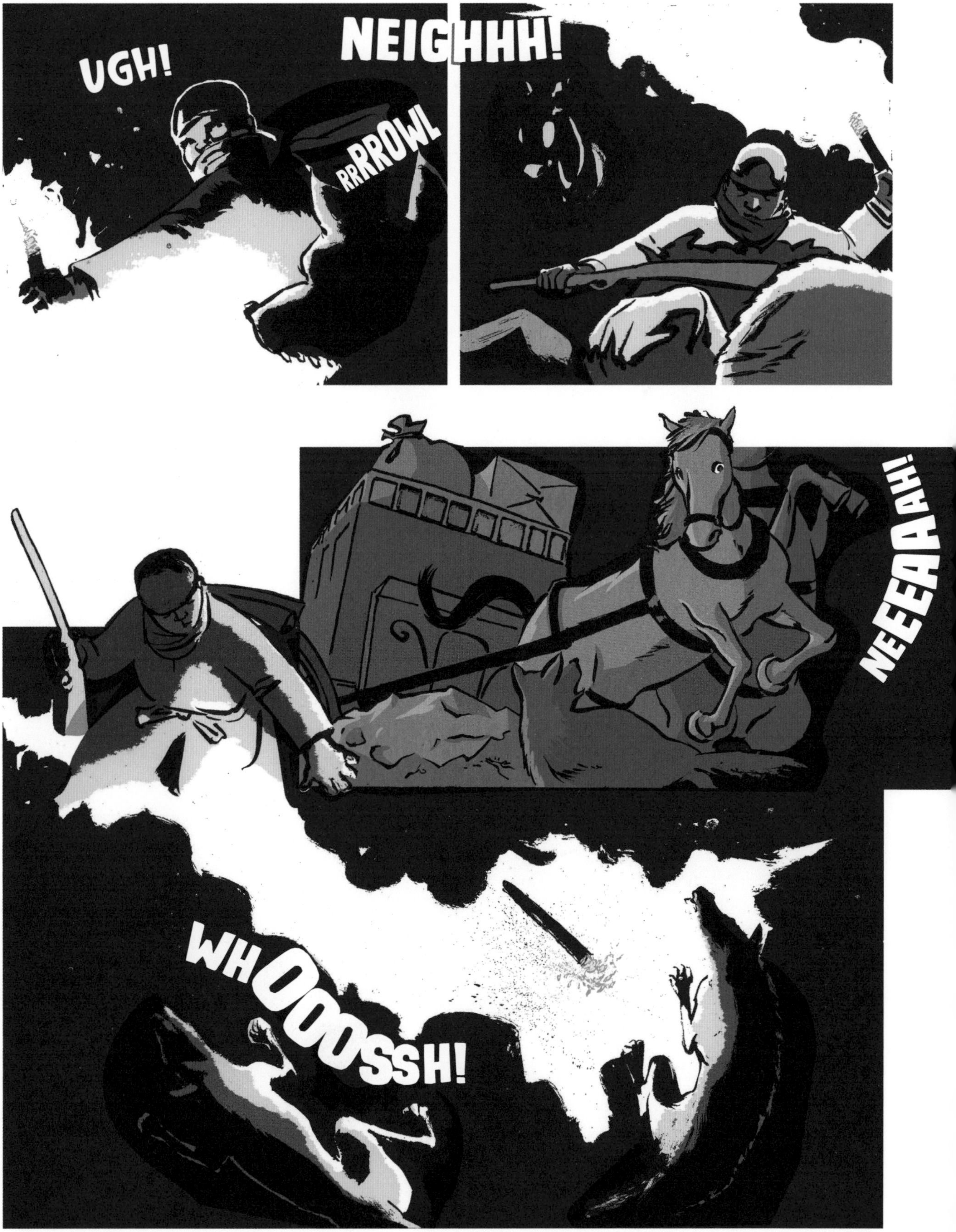
UGH!
NEIGHHH!
RRRROWL
NEEEAAAH!
WHOOOSSH!

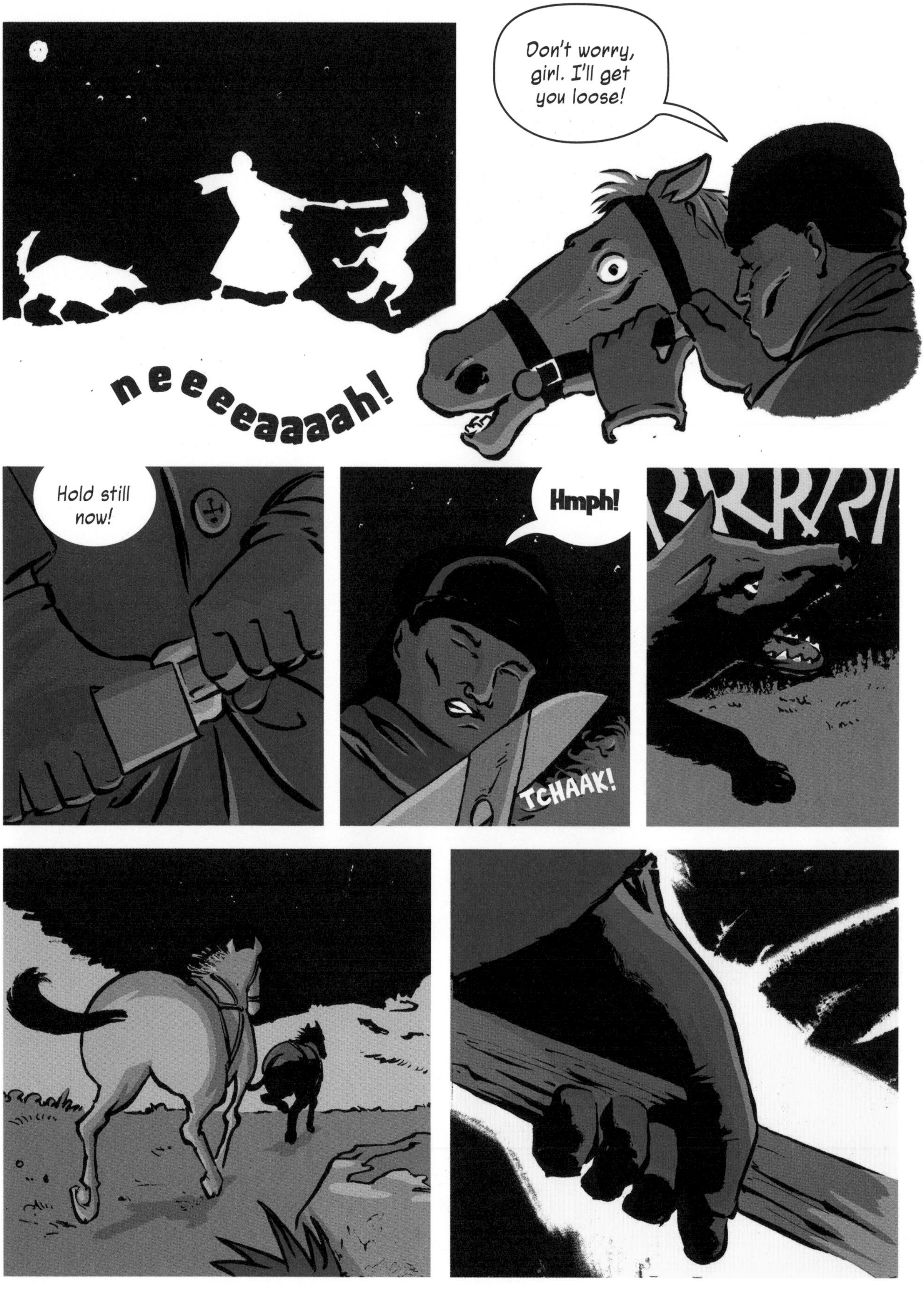

Don't worry, girl. I'll get you loose!
neeeeaaaah!
Hold still now!
Hmph!
TCHAAK!
RRRR!

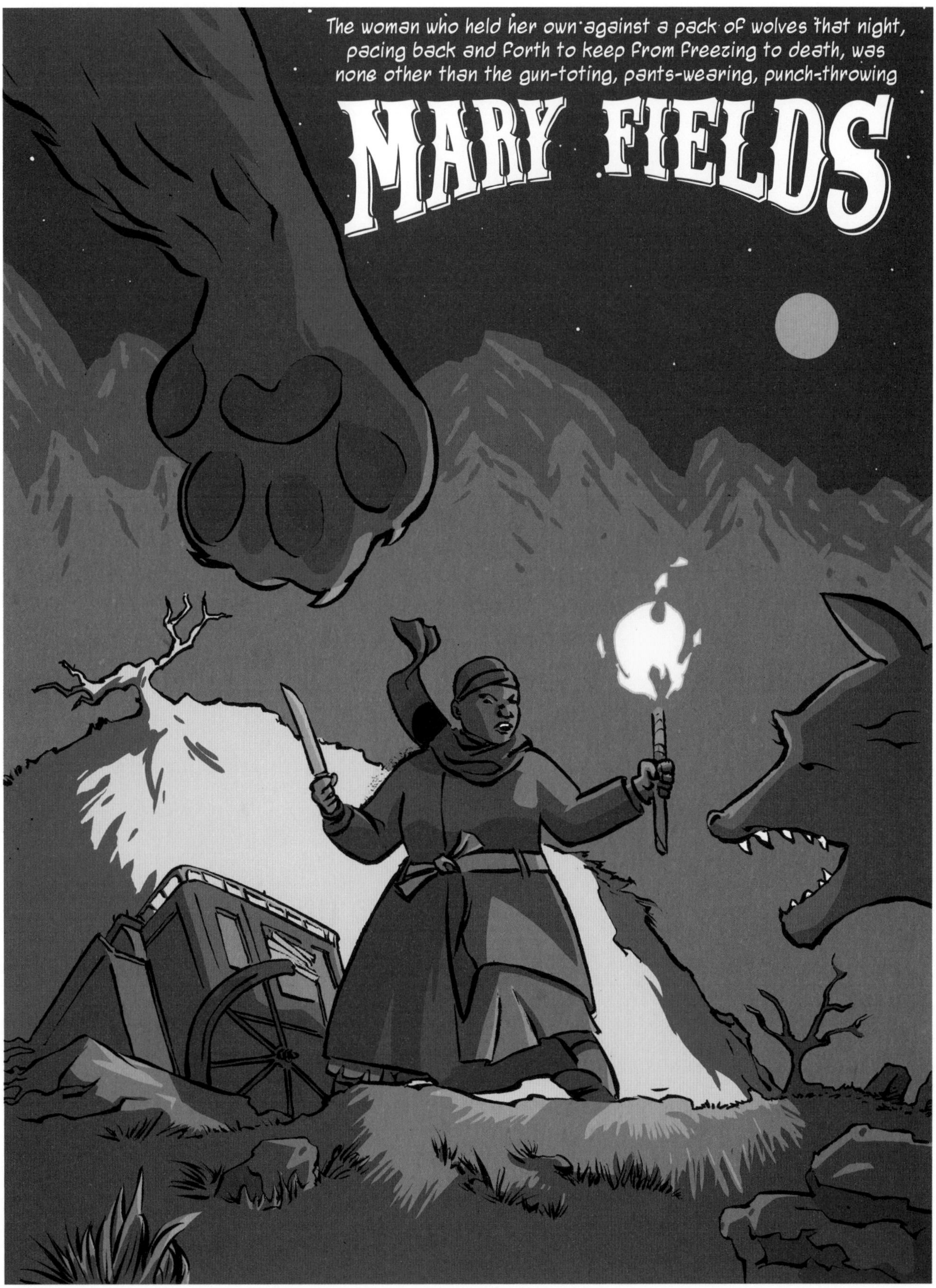
The woman who held her own against a pack of wolves that night, pacing back and forth to keep from freezing to death, was none other than the gun-toting, pants-wearing, punch-throwing
MARY FIELDS

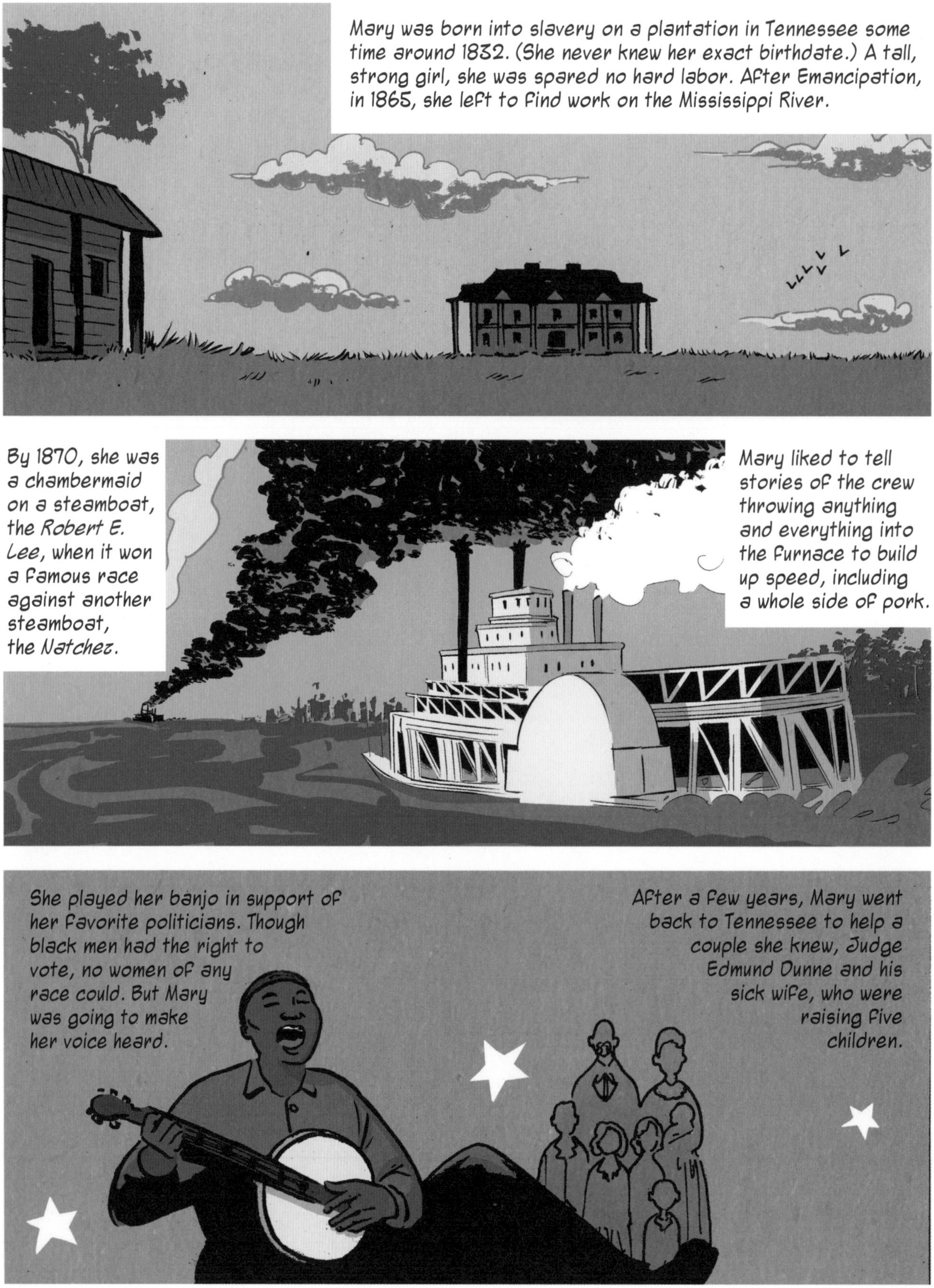
Mary was born into slavery on a plantation in Tennessee some time around 1832. (She never knew her exact birthdate.) A tall, strong girl, she was spared no hard labor. After Emancipation, in 1865, she left to find work on the Mississippi River.
By 1870, she was a chambermaid on a steamboat, the *Robert E. Lee*, when it won a famous race against another steamboat, the *Natchez*.
Mary liked to tell stories of the crew throwing anything and everything into the furnace to build up speed, including a whole side of pork.
She played her banjo in support of her favorite politicians. Though black men had the right to vote, no women of any race could. But Mary was going to make her voice heard.
After a few years, Mary went back to Tennessee to help a couple she knew, Judge Edmund Dunne and his sick wife, who were raising five children.

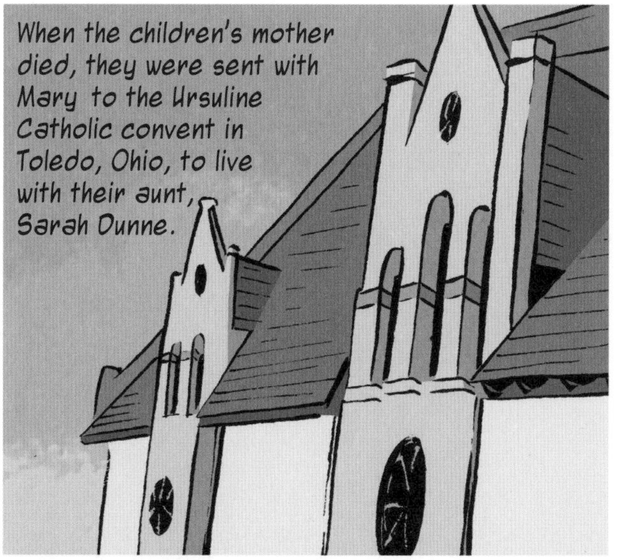
When the children's mother died, they were sent with Mary to the Ursuline Catholic convent in Toledo, Ohio, to live with their aunt, Sarah Dunne.

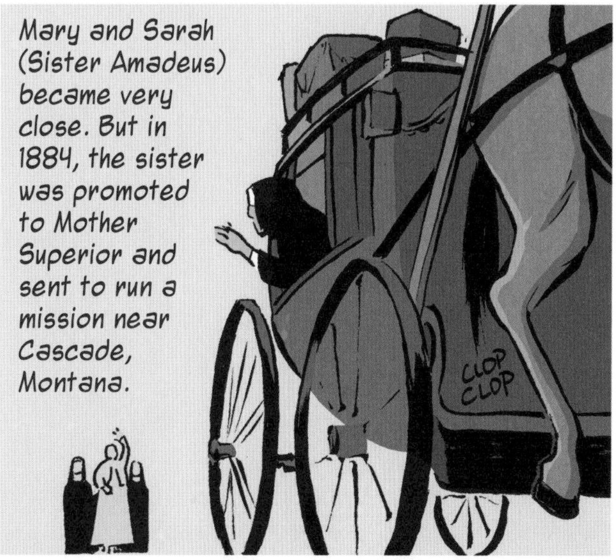
Mary and Sarah (Sister Amadeus) became very close. But in 1884, the sister was promoted to Mother Superior and sent to run a mission near Cascade, Montana.
CLOP
CLOP

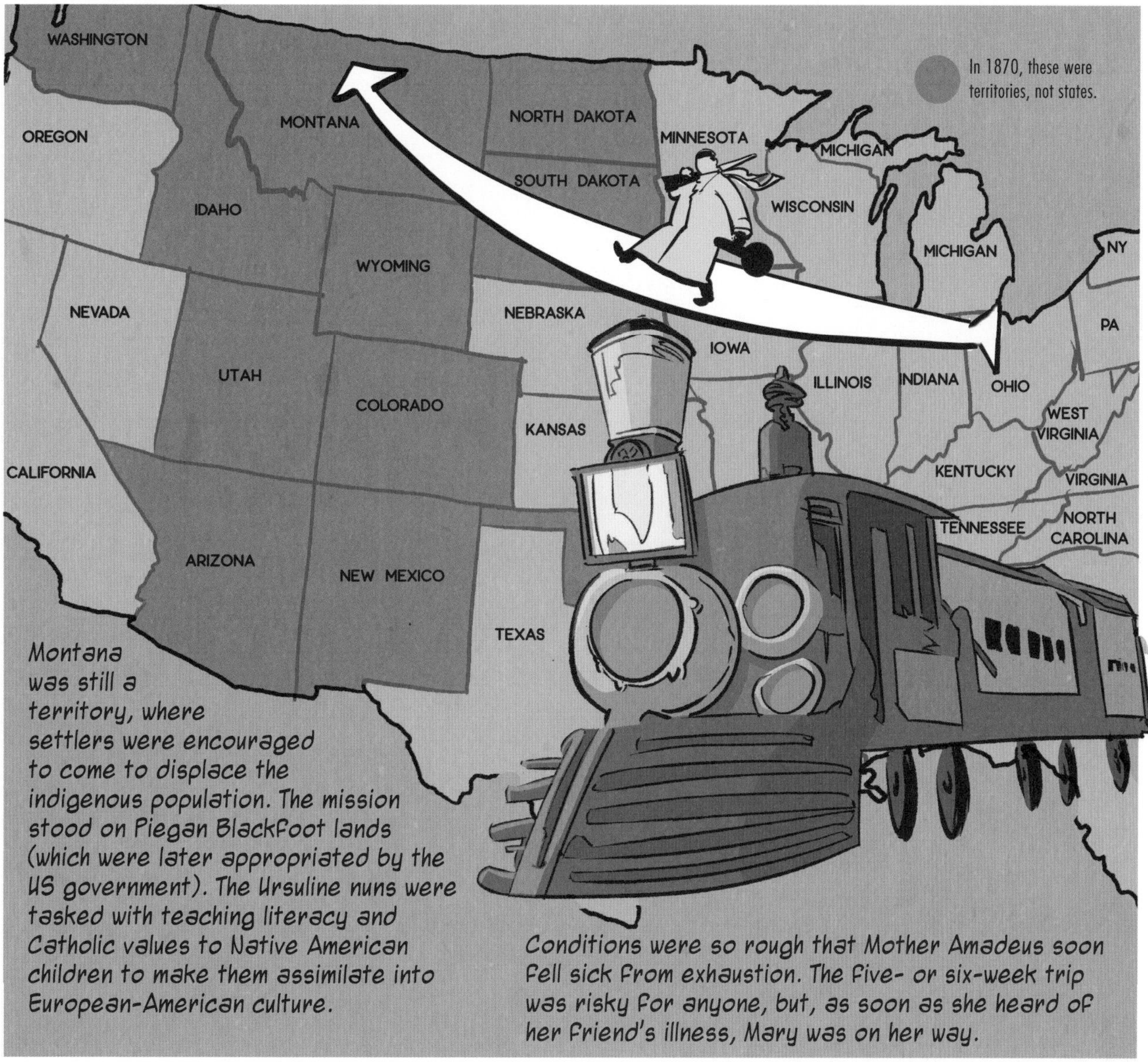
In 1870, these were territories, not states.
WASHINGTON
OREGON
MONTANA
NORTH DAKOTA
SOUTH DAKOTA
MINNESOTA
MICHIGAN
WISCONSIN
MICHIGAN
NY
IDAHO
WYOMING
NEVADA
NEBRASKA
PA
IOWA
UTAH
ILLINOIS
INDIANA
OHIO
COLORADO
KANSAS
WEST VIRGINIA
CALIFORNIA
KENTUCKY
VIRGINIA
TENNESSEE
NORTH CAROLINA
ARIZONA
NEW MEXICO
TEXAS
Montana was still a territory, where settlers were encouraged to come to displace the indigenous population. The mission stood on Piegan Blackfoot lands (which were later appropriated by the US government). The Ursuline nuns were tasked with teaching literacy and Catholic values to Native American children to make them assimilate into European-American culture.
Conditions were so rough that Mother Amadeus soon fell sick from exhaustion. The five- or six-week trip was risky for anyone, but, as soon as she heard of her friend's illness, Mary was on her way.

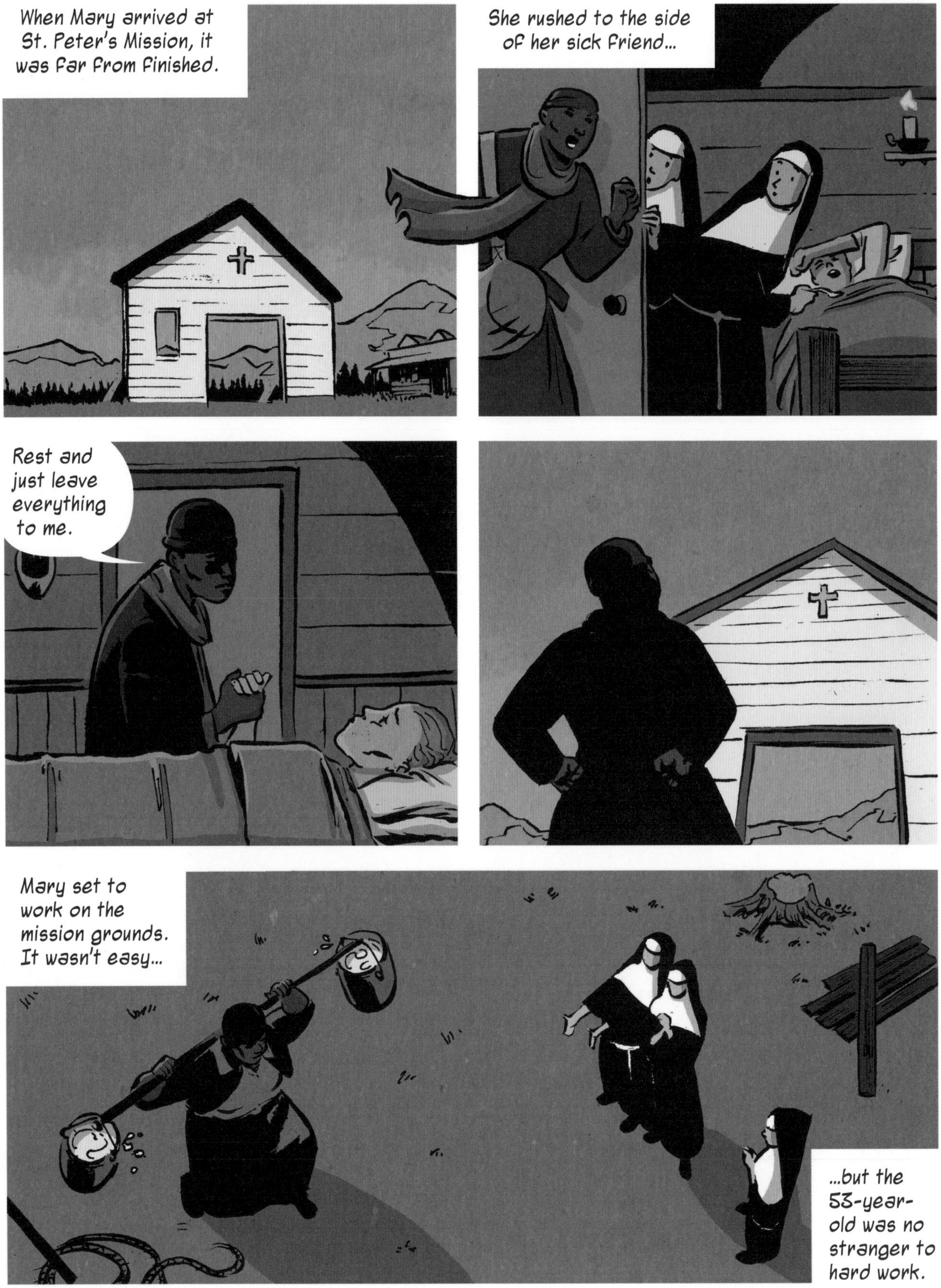
When Mary arrived at St. Peter's Mission, it was far from finished.
She rushed to the side of her sick friend...
Rest and just leave everything to me.
Mary set to work on the mission grounds. It wasn't easy...
...but the 53-year-old was no stranger to hard work.

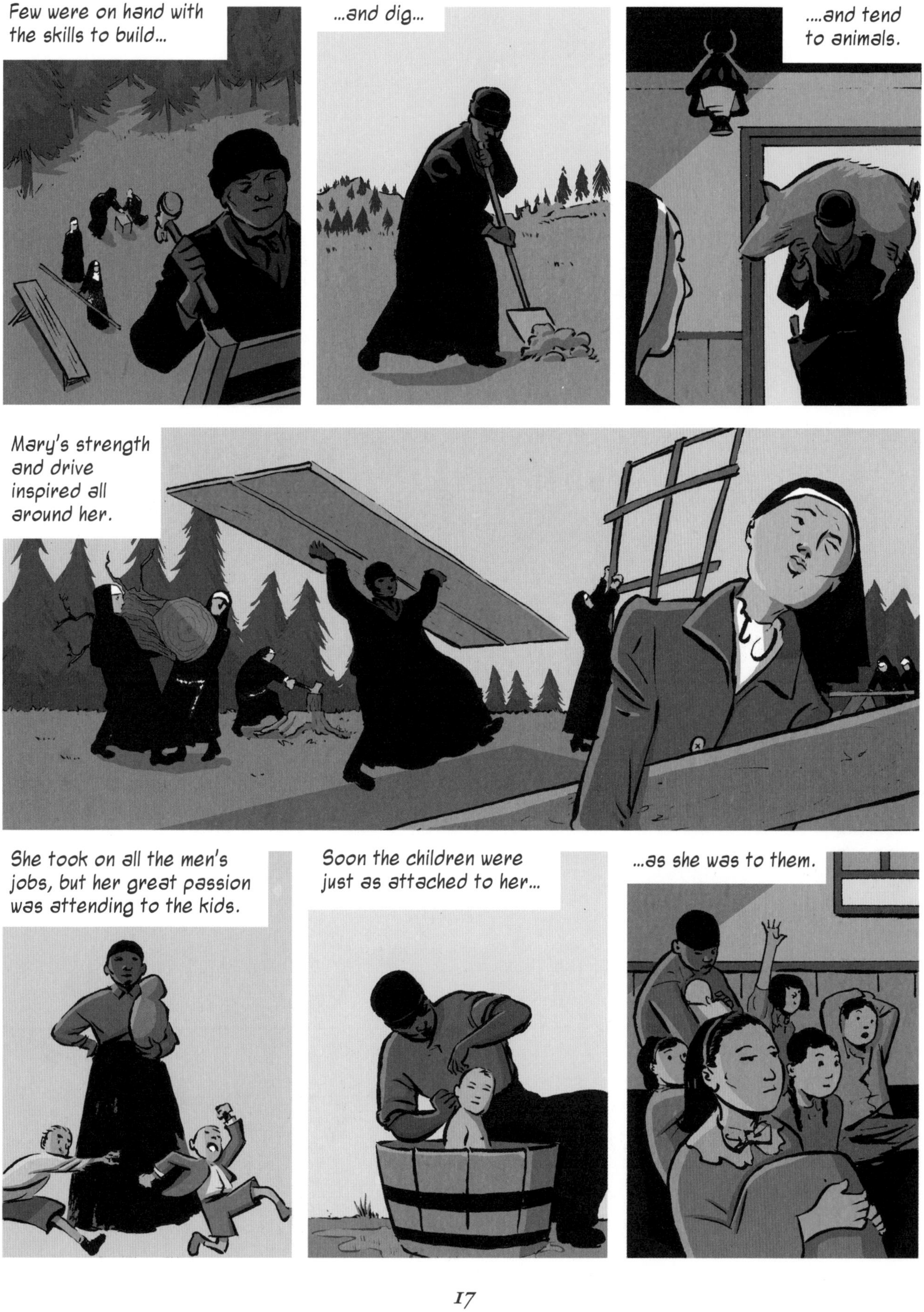
Few were on hand with the skills to build...
...and dig...
....and tend to animals.
Mary's strength and drive inspired all around her.
She took on all the men's jobs, but her great passion was attending to the kids.
Soon the children were just as attached to her...
...as she was to them.

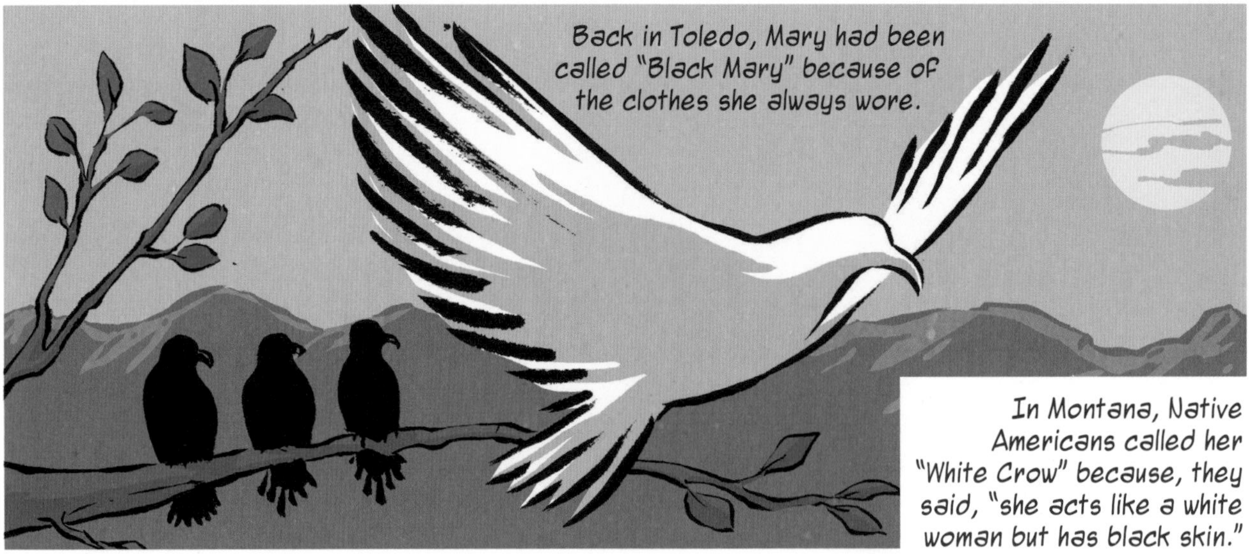
Back in Toledo, Mary had been called "Black Mary" because of the clothes she always wore.
In Montana, Native Americans called her "White Crow" because, they said, "she acts like a white woman but has black skin."

In fact, as the only woman allowed in any of the many saloons of nearby Cascade, she demanded - and got - the respect usually reserved for white men.

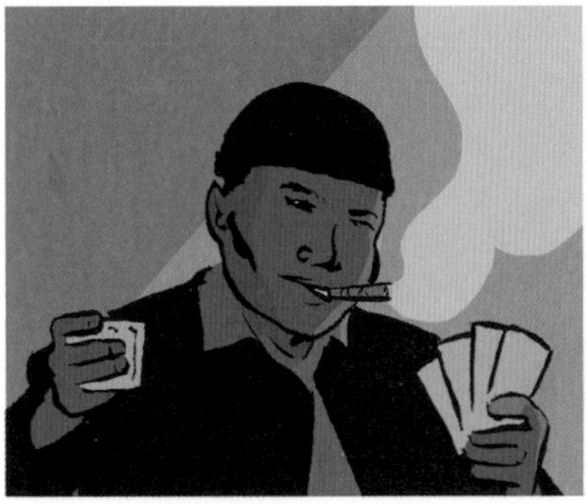

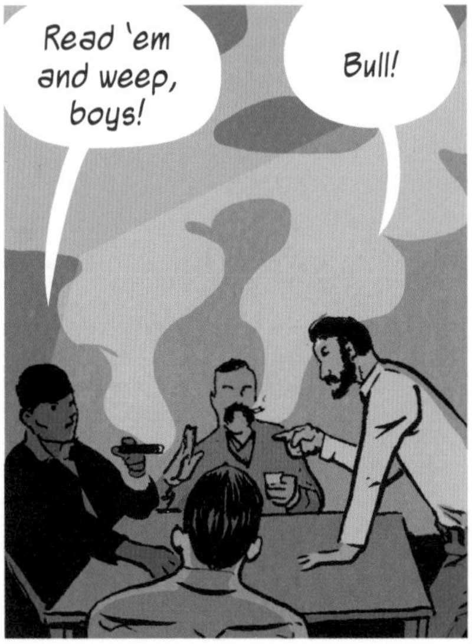
Read 'em and weep, boys!
Bull!

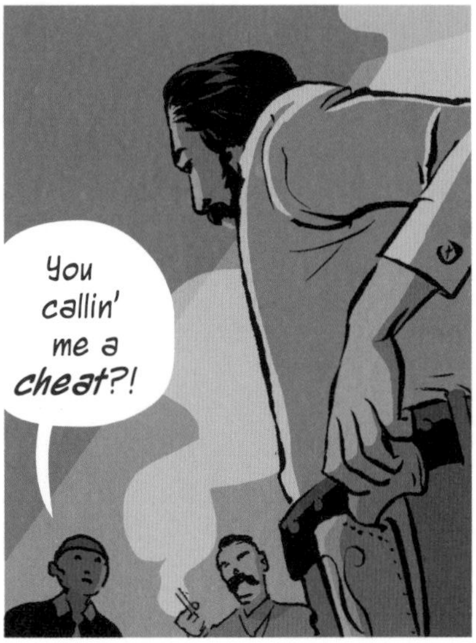
You callin' me a *cheat*?!

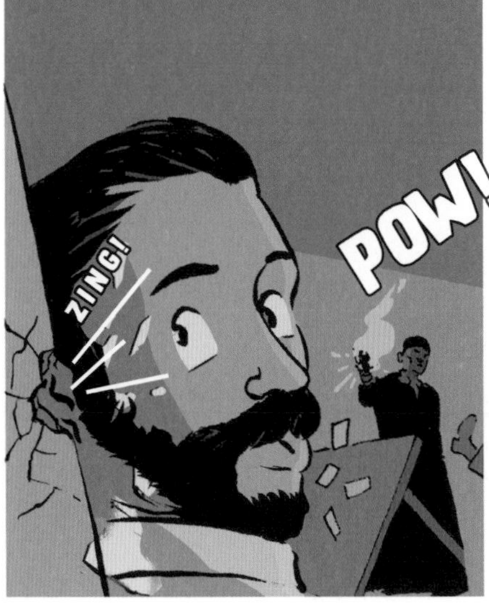
ZING!
POW!

News of Mary's gunplay didn't please Montana's bishop, John Brondell.

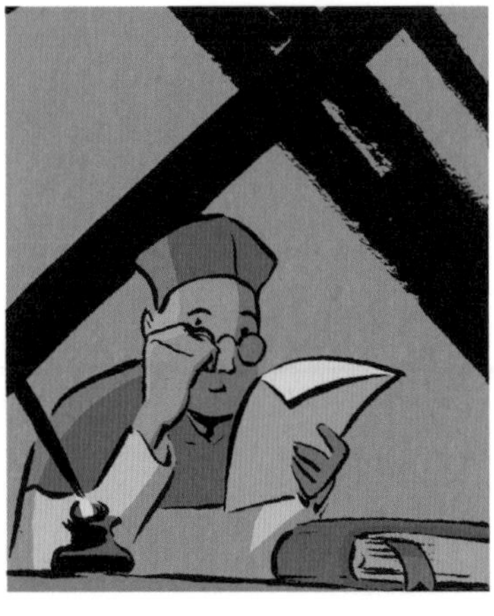

In 1894, after ten years of unswerving devotion, Mary was told to leave the mission.

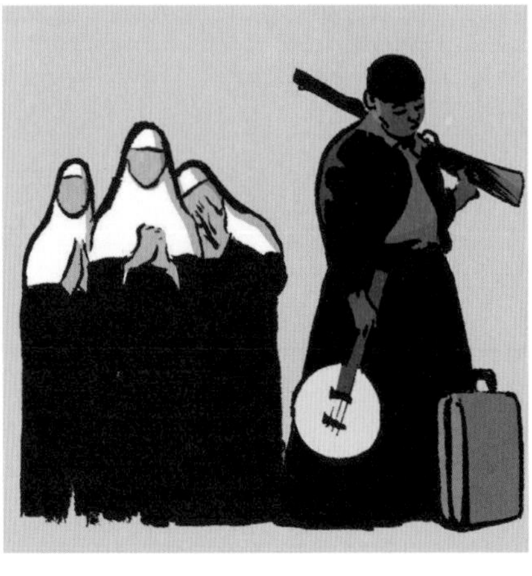

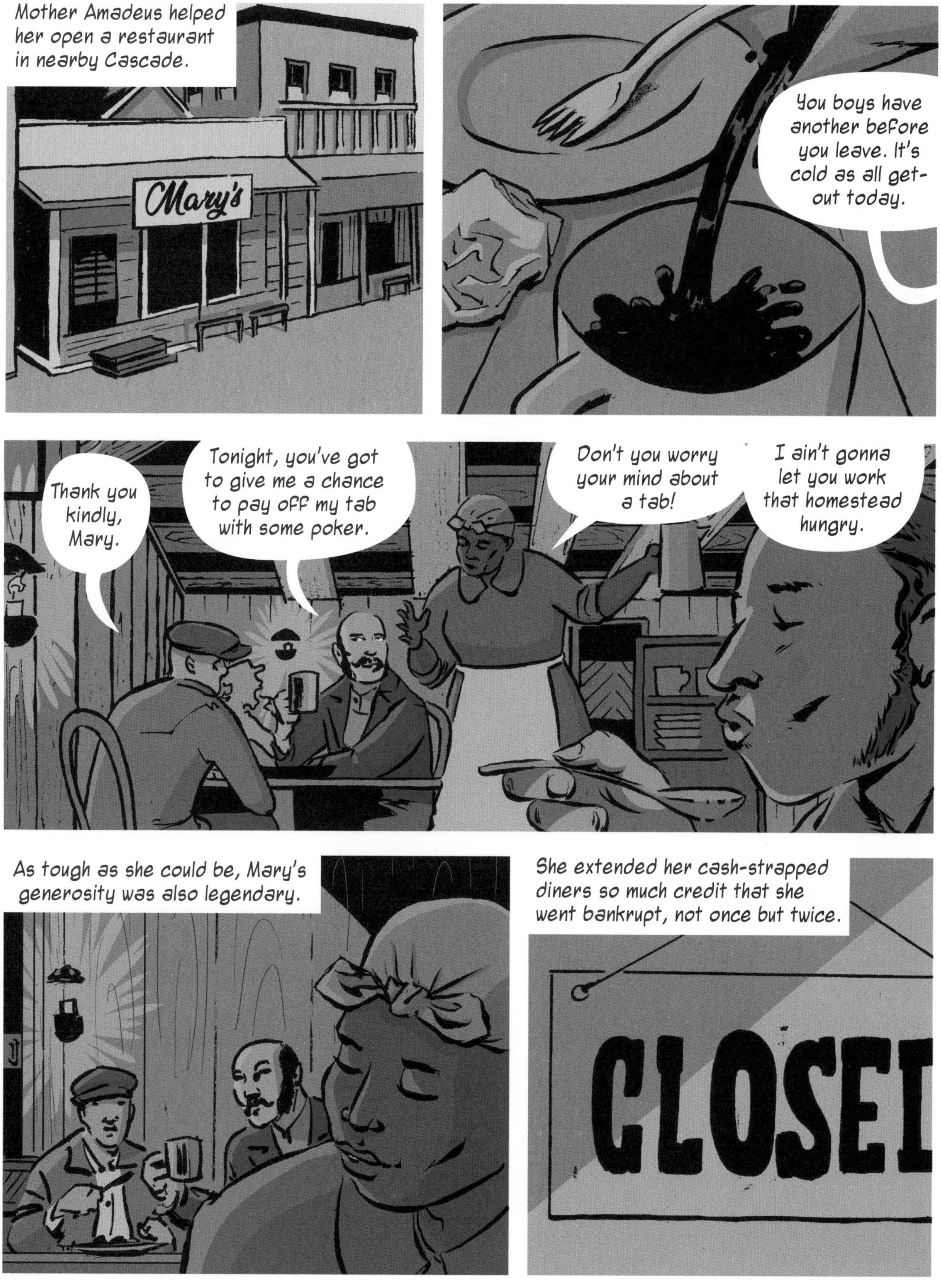
Mother Amadeus helped her open a restaurant in nearby Cascade.
Mary's
You boys have another before you leave. It's cold as all get-out today.
Thank you kindly, Mary.
Tonight, you've got to give me a chance to pay off my tab with some poker.
Don't you worry your mind about a tab!
I ain't gonna let you work that homestead hungry.
As tough as she could be, Mary's generosity was also legendary.
She extended her cash-strapped diners so much credit that she went bankrupt, not once but twice.
CLOSEI

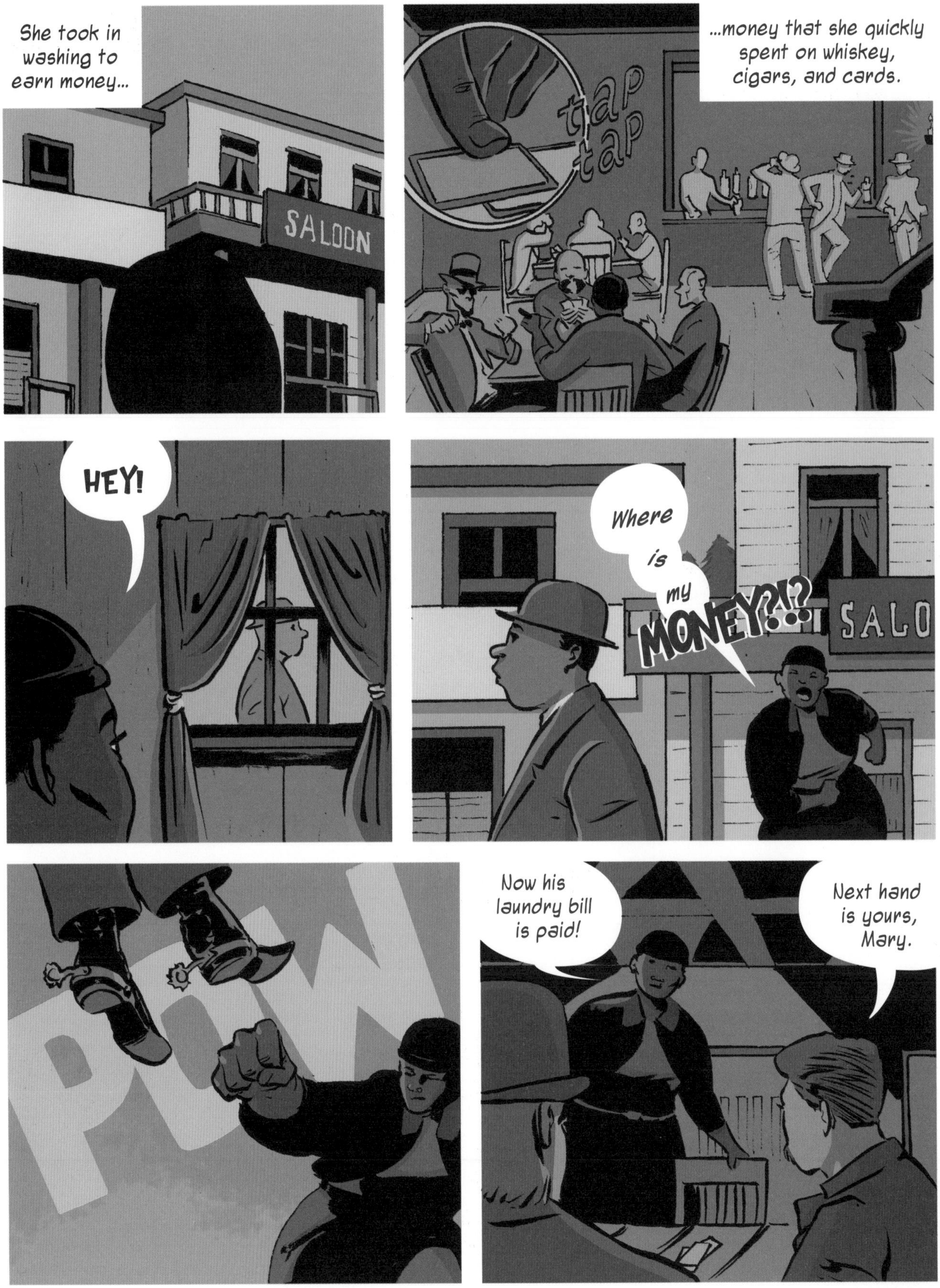
She took in washing to earn money...
SALOON
...money that she quickly spent on whiskey, cigars, and cards.
tap tap
HEY!
Where is my MONEY?!?
SALO
POW
Now his laundry bill is paid!
Next hand is yours, Mary.

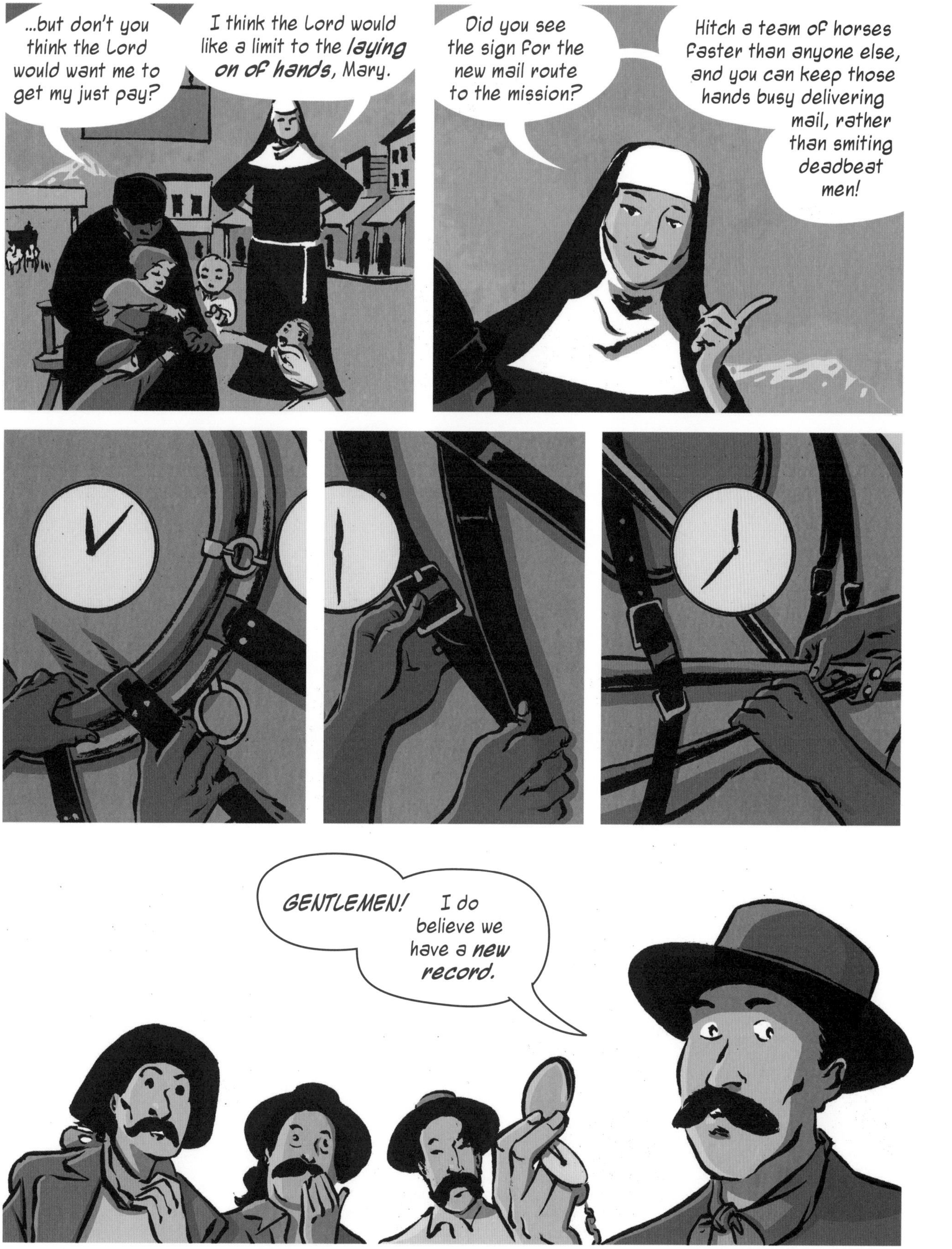
...but don't you think the Lord would want me to get my just pay?
I think the Lord would like a limit to the *laying on of hands*, Mary.
Did you see the sign for the new mail route to the mission?
Hitch a team of horses faster than anyone else, and you can keep those hands busy delivering mail, rather than smiting deadbeat men!
GENTLEMEN! I do believe we have a *new record.*

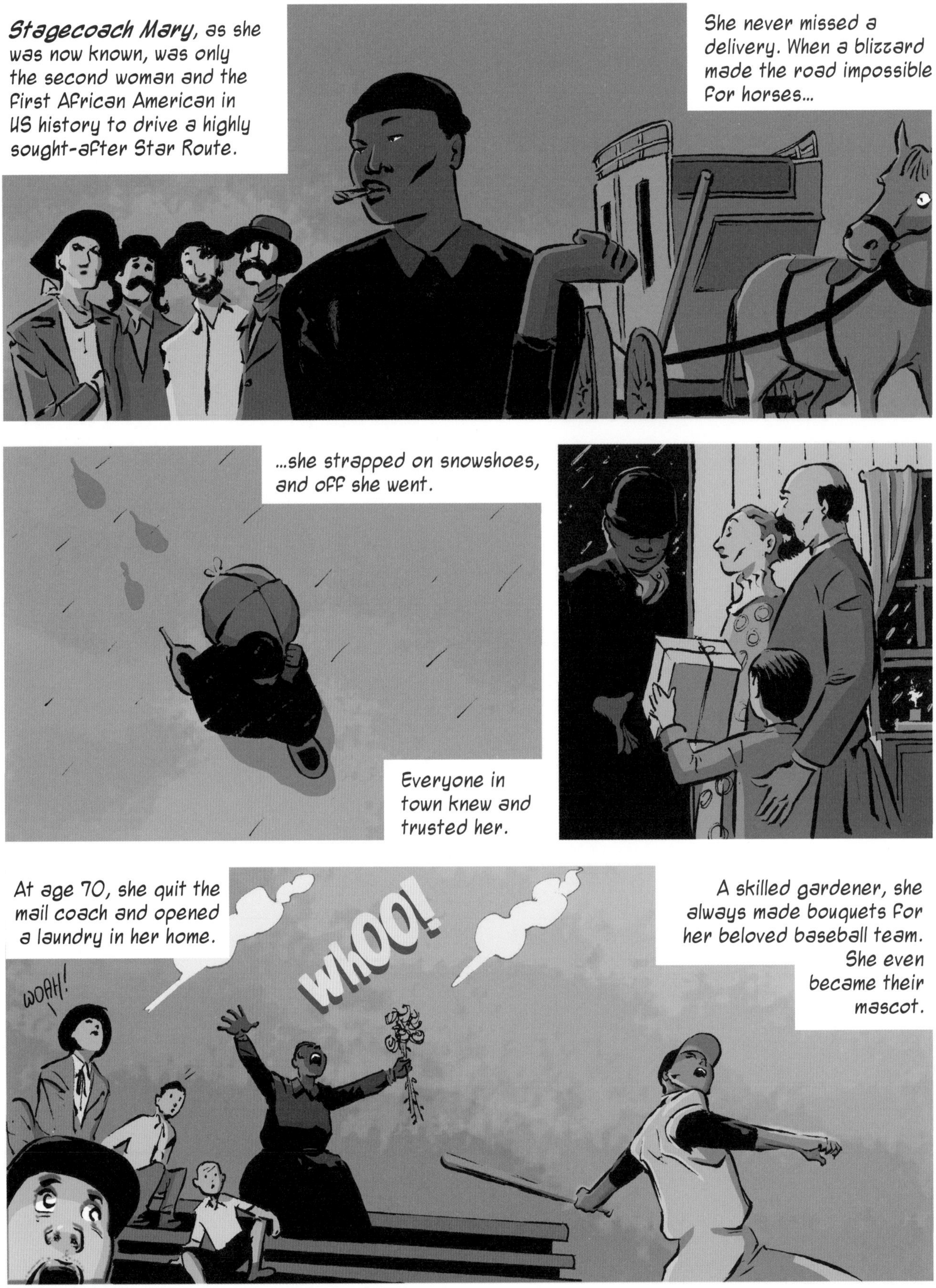
Stagecoach Mary, as she was now known, was only the second woman and the first African American in US history to drive a highly sought-after Star Route.
She never missed a delivery. When a blizzard made the road impossible for horses...
...she strapped on snowshoes, and off she went.
Everyone in town knew and trusted her.
At age 70, she quit the mail coach and opened a laundry in her home.
WOAH!
WhOO!
A skilled gardener, she always made bouquets for her beloved baseball team. She even became their mascot.

Because she was born enslaved, Mary never knew her exact birthday.

She was so loved in Cascade that the school would close and the town would celebrate whatever dates she'd come up with, **once or twice** a year.

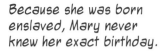

HAPPY BIRTHDAY

The actor Gary Cooper, who remembered meeting her when he was a nine-year-old boy, said: "She may have been born a slave, but she lived to become one of the freest souls ever to draw a breath... or a .38!"

Black Mary, White Crow, Stagecoach Mary... Who was Mary Fields?

Whoever she wanted to be!

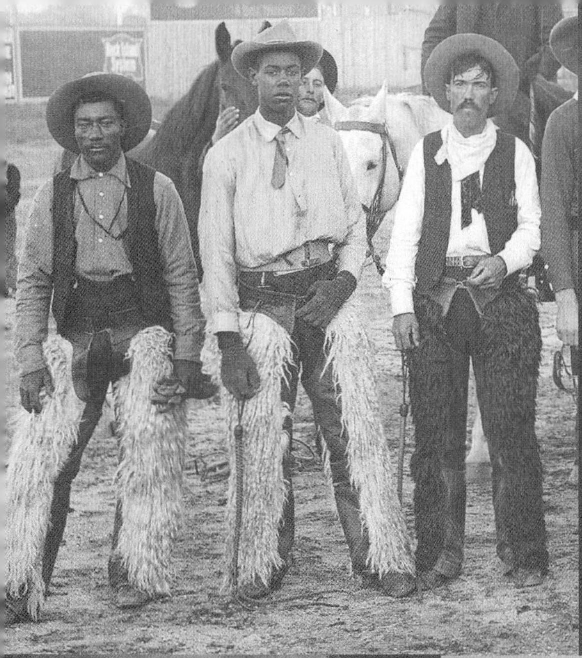
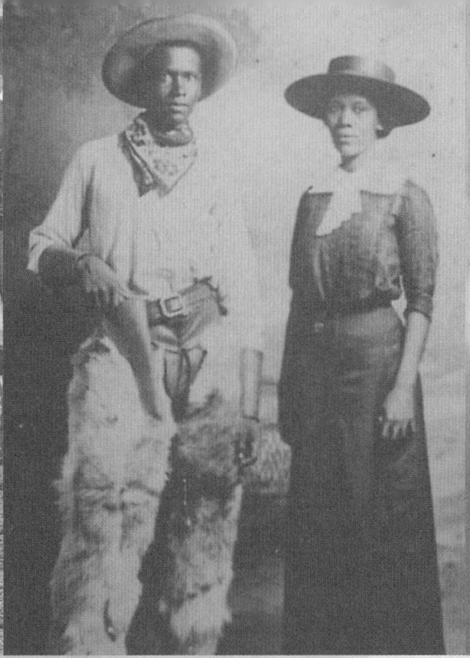
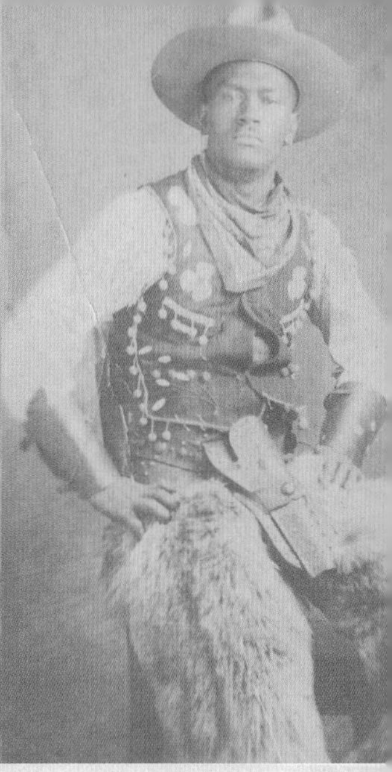
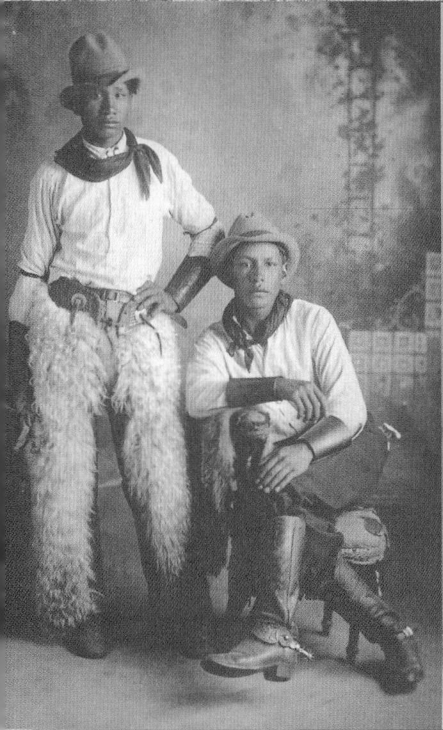
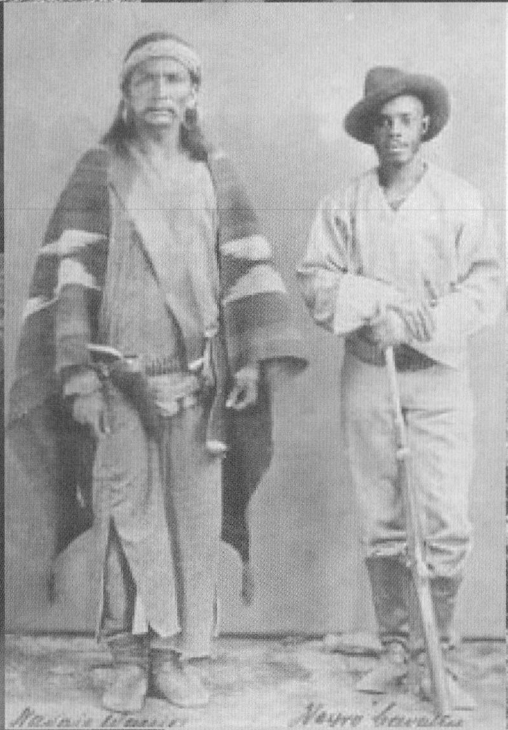
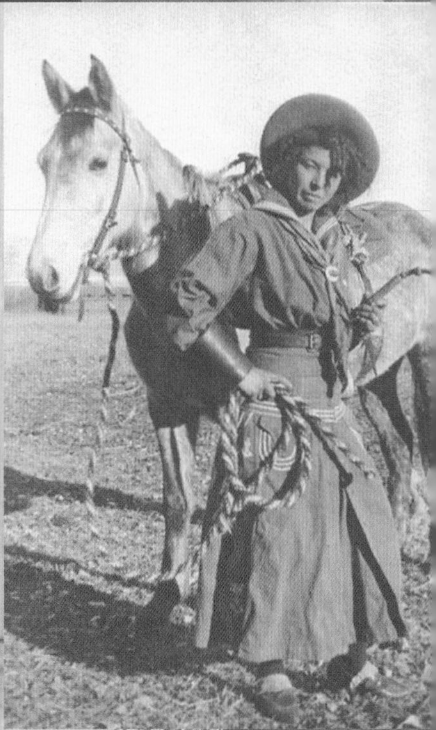
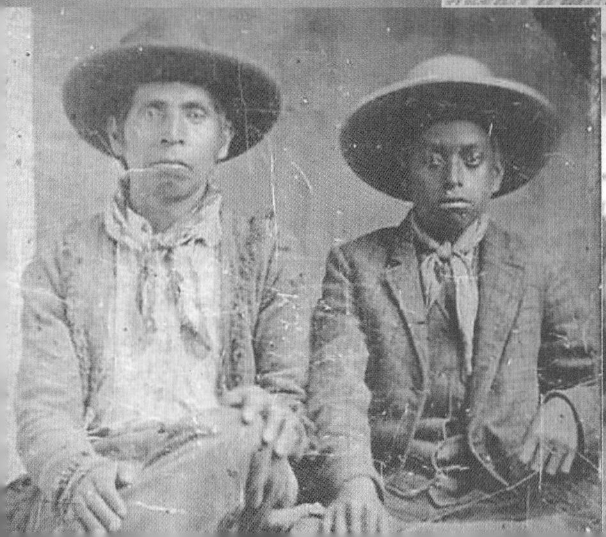
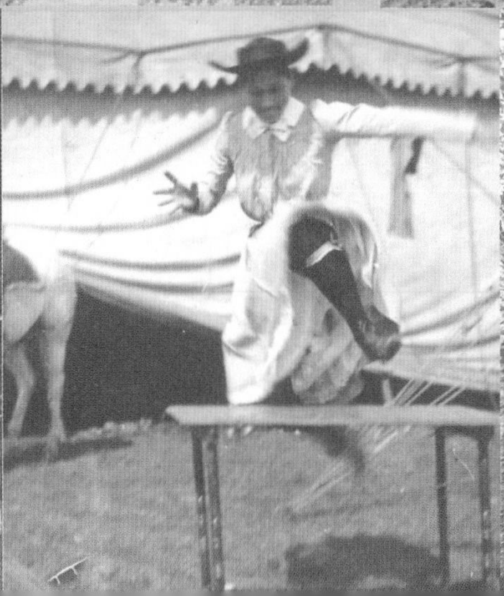
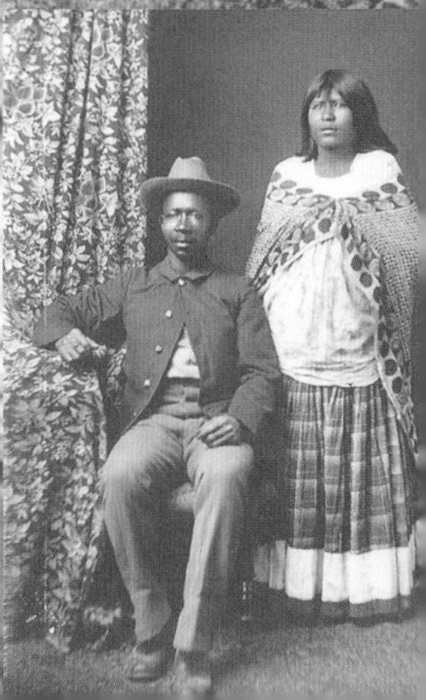

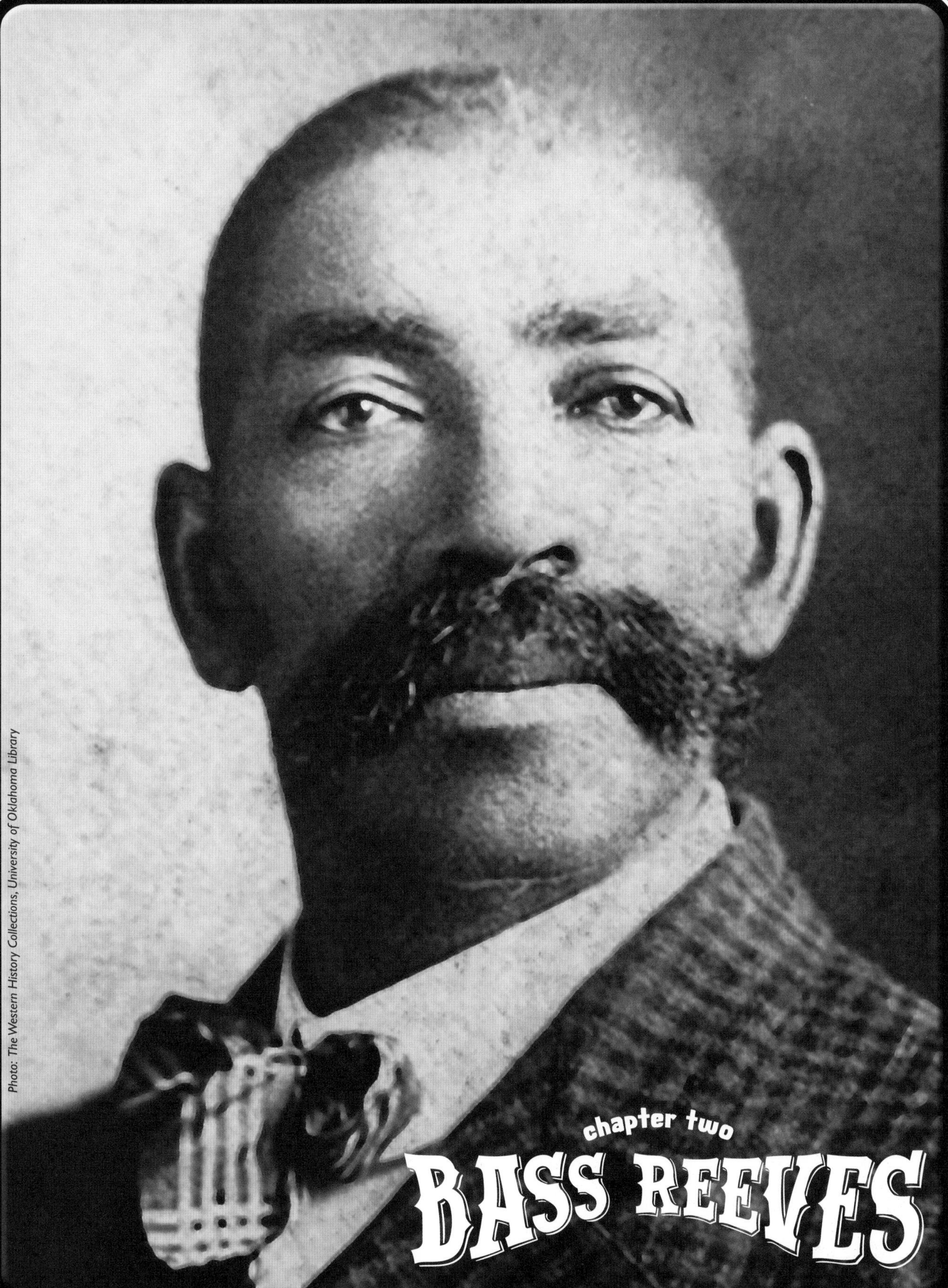

Photo: The Western History Collections, University of Oklahoma Library

chapter two

BASS REEVES

In Arkansas, our second hero was a legend in his own time...

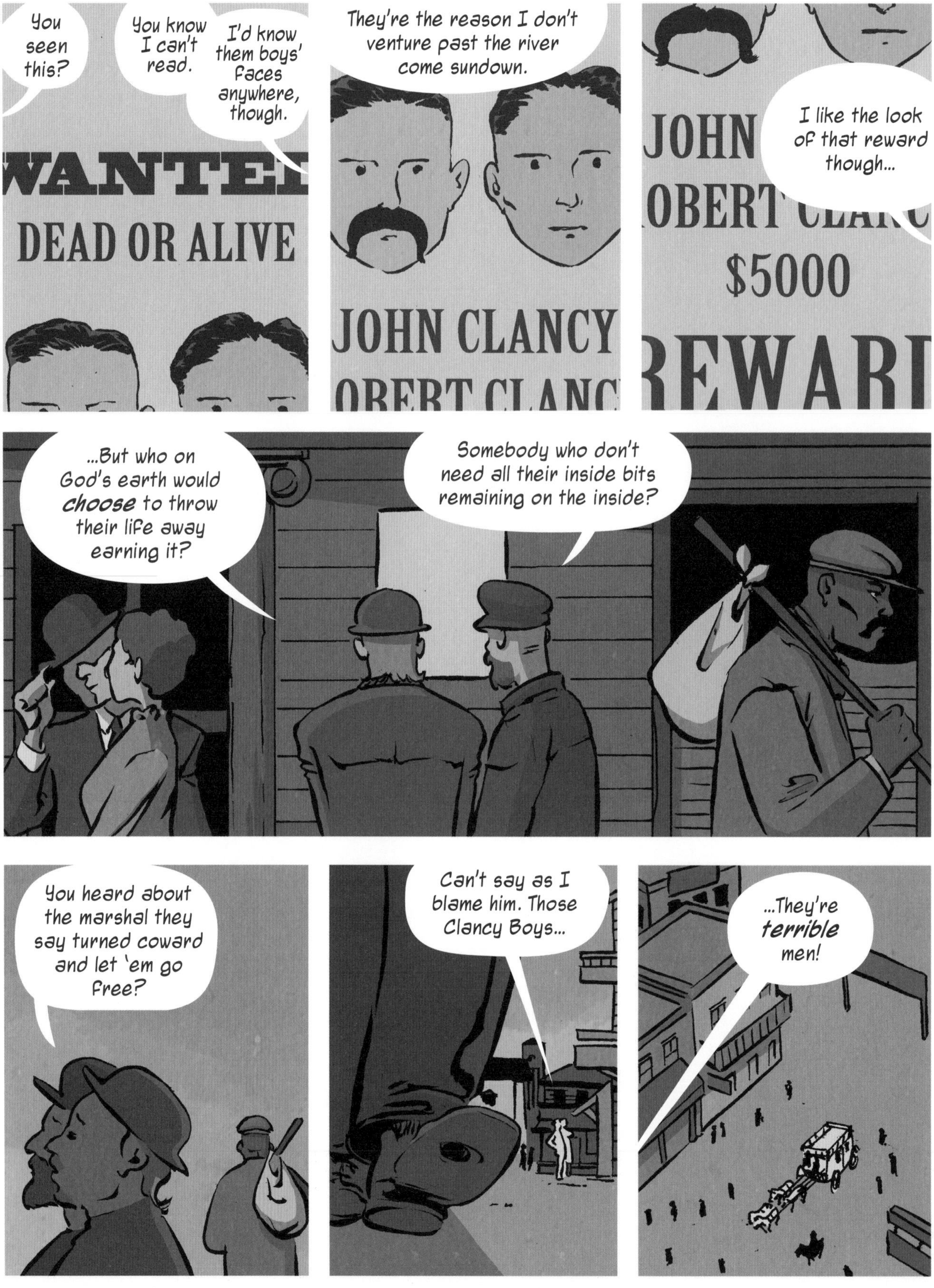

You seen this?
You know I can't read.
I'd know them boys' faces anywhere, though.
WANTED
DEAD OR ALIVE
They're the reason I don't venture past the river come sundown.
JOHN CLANCY
OBERT CLANC
JOHN
OBERT CLANC
$5000
REWARD
I like the look of that reward though...
...But who on God's earth would ***choose*** to throw their life away earning it?
Somebody who don't need all their inside bits remaining on the inside?
You heard about the marshal they say turned coward and let 'em go free?
Can't say as I blame him. Those Clancy Boys...
...They're ***terrible*** men!

BASS REEVES

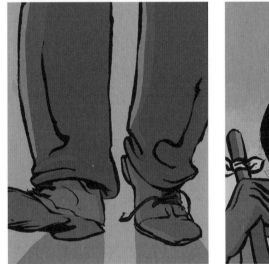

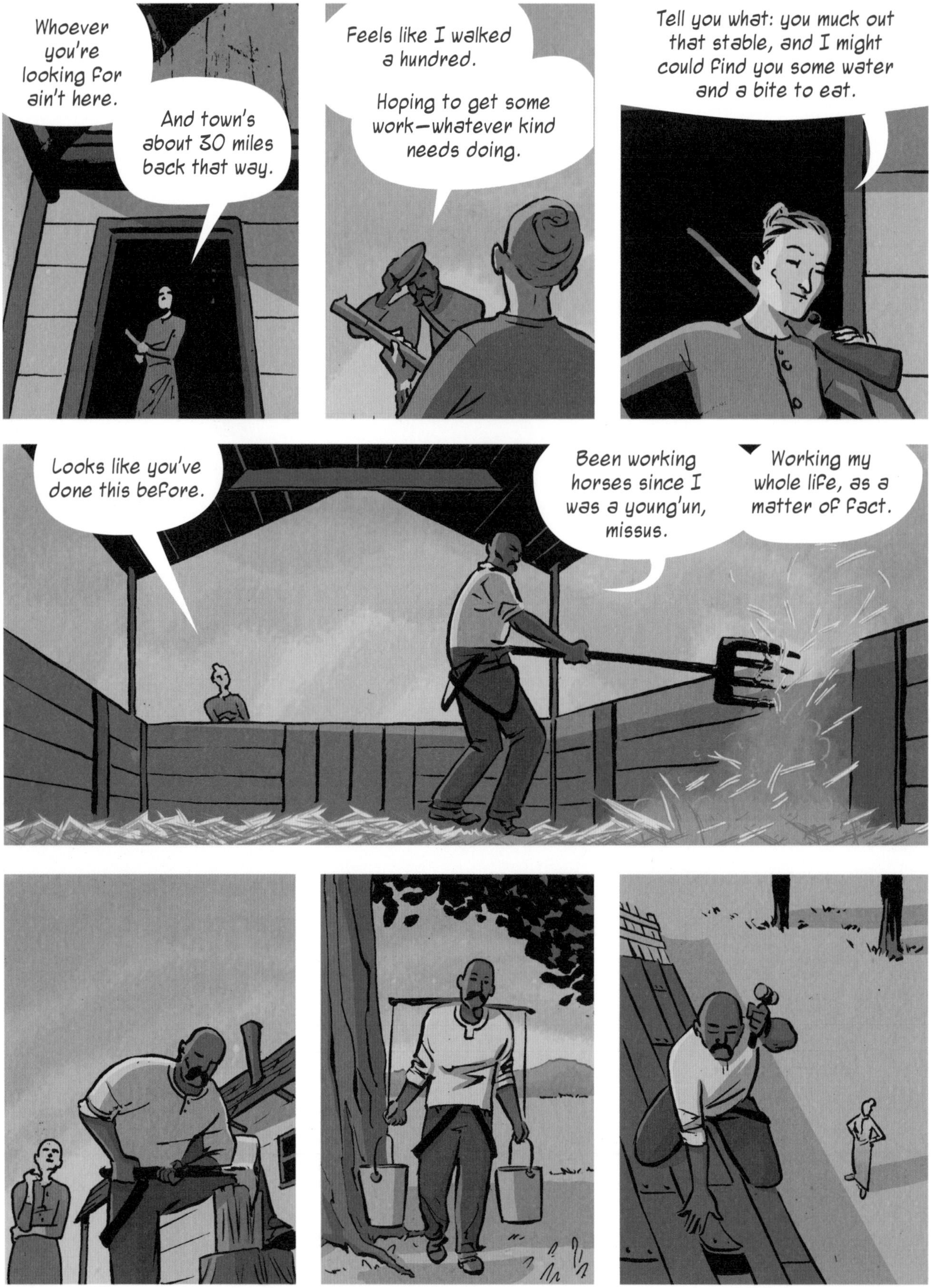

Whoever you're looking for ain't here.
And town's about 30 miles back that way.
Feels like I walked a hundred.
Hoping to get some work—whatever kind needs doing.
Tell you what: you muck out that stable, and I might could find you some water and a bite to eat.
Looks like you've done this before.
Been working horses since I was a young'un, missus.
Working my whole life, as a matter of fact.

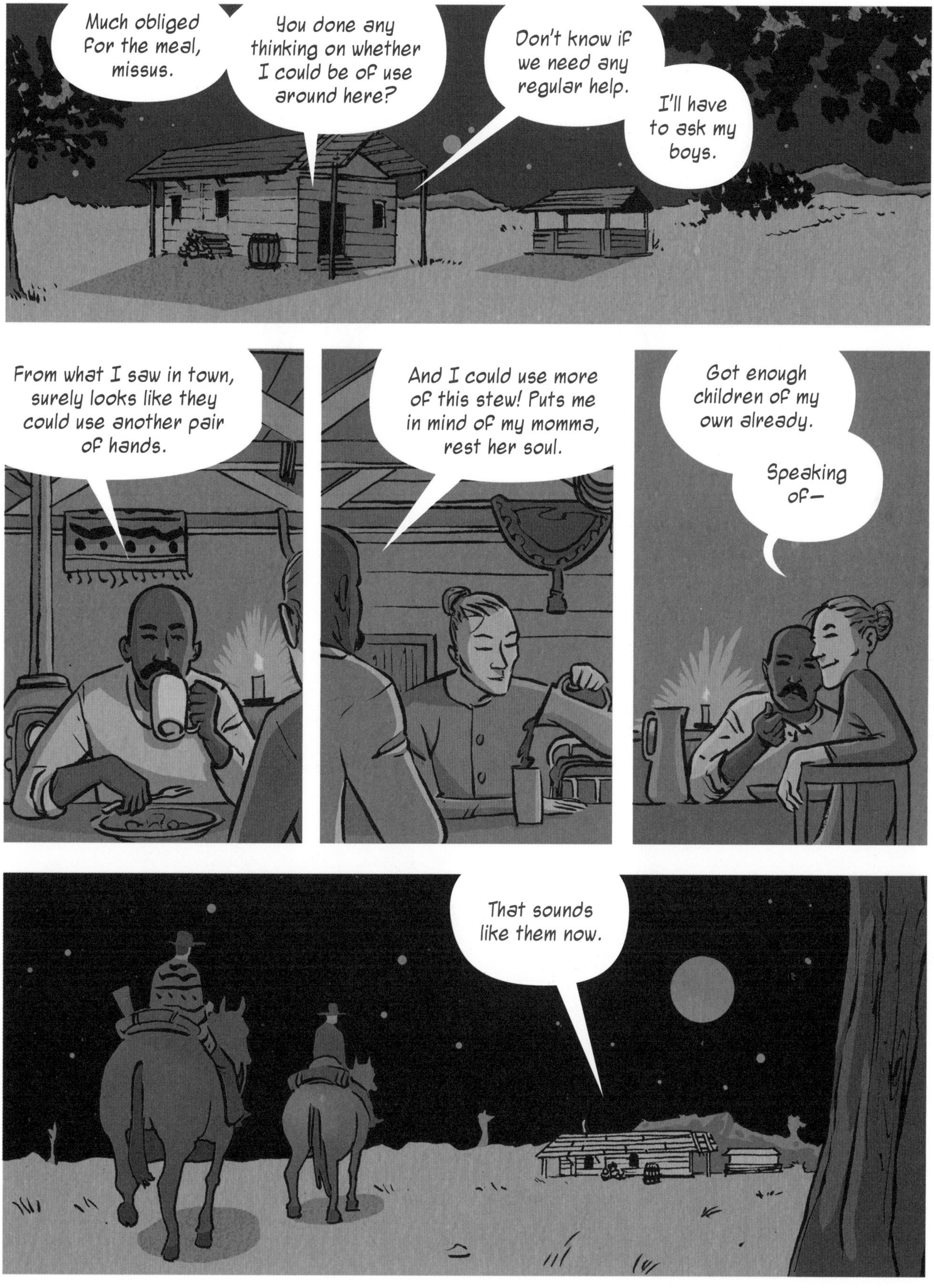
Much obliged for the meal, missus.
You done any thinking on whether I could be of use around here?
Don't know if we need any regular help.
I'll have to ask my boys.
From what I saw in town, surely looks like they could use another pair of hands.
And I could use more of this stew! Puts me in mind of my momma, rest her soul.
Got enough children of my own already.
Speaking of—
That sounds like them now.

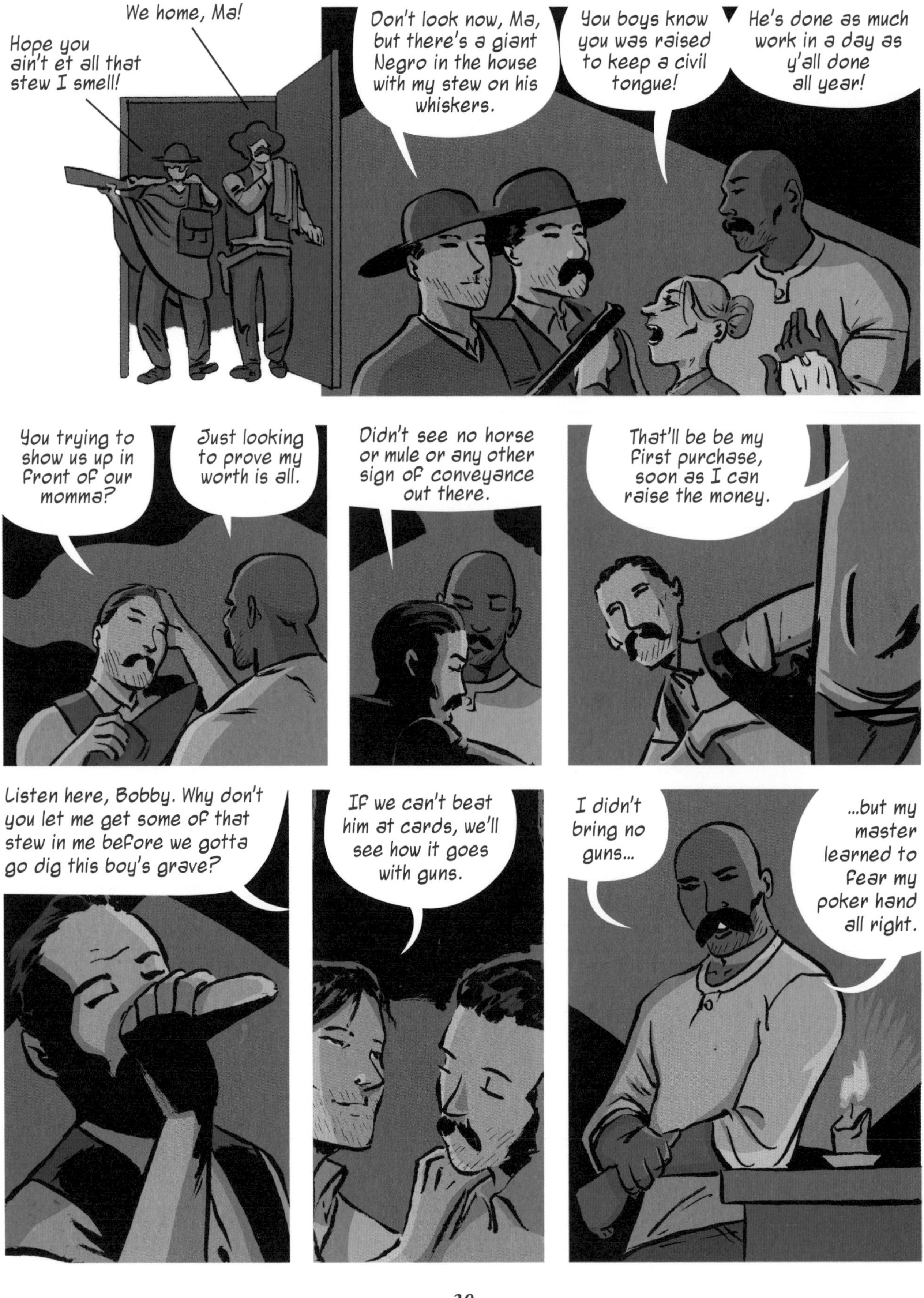
We home, Ma!
Hope you ain't et all that stew I smell!
Don't look now, Ma, but there's a giant Negro in the house with my stew on his whiskers.
You boys know you was raised to keep a civil tongue!
He's done as much work in a day as y'all done all year!
You trying to show us up in front of our momma?
Just looking to prove my worth is all.
Didn't see no horse or mule or any other sign of conveyance out there.
That'll be be my first purchase, soon as I can raise the money.
Listen here, Bobby. Why don't you let me get some of that stew in me before we gotta go dig this boy's grave?
If we can't beat him at cards, we'll see how it goes with guns.
I didn't bring no guns...
...but my master learned to fear my poker hand all right.

It's your play, boy.

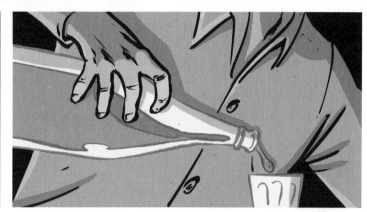

Pardon. I'm just thinking about how to ask you gentlemen a question.

You plan on askin' it before or after the Second Coming?

That's what passes for a civil tongue in these parts?

You still breathin', ain't you?

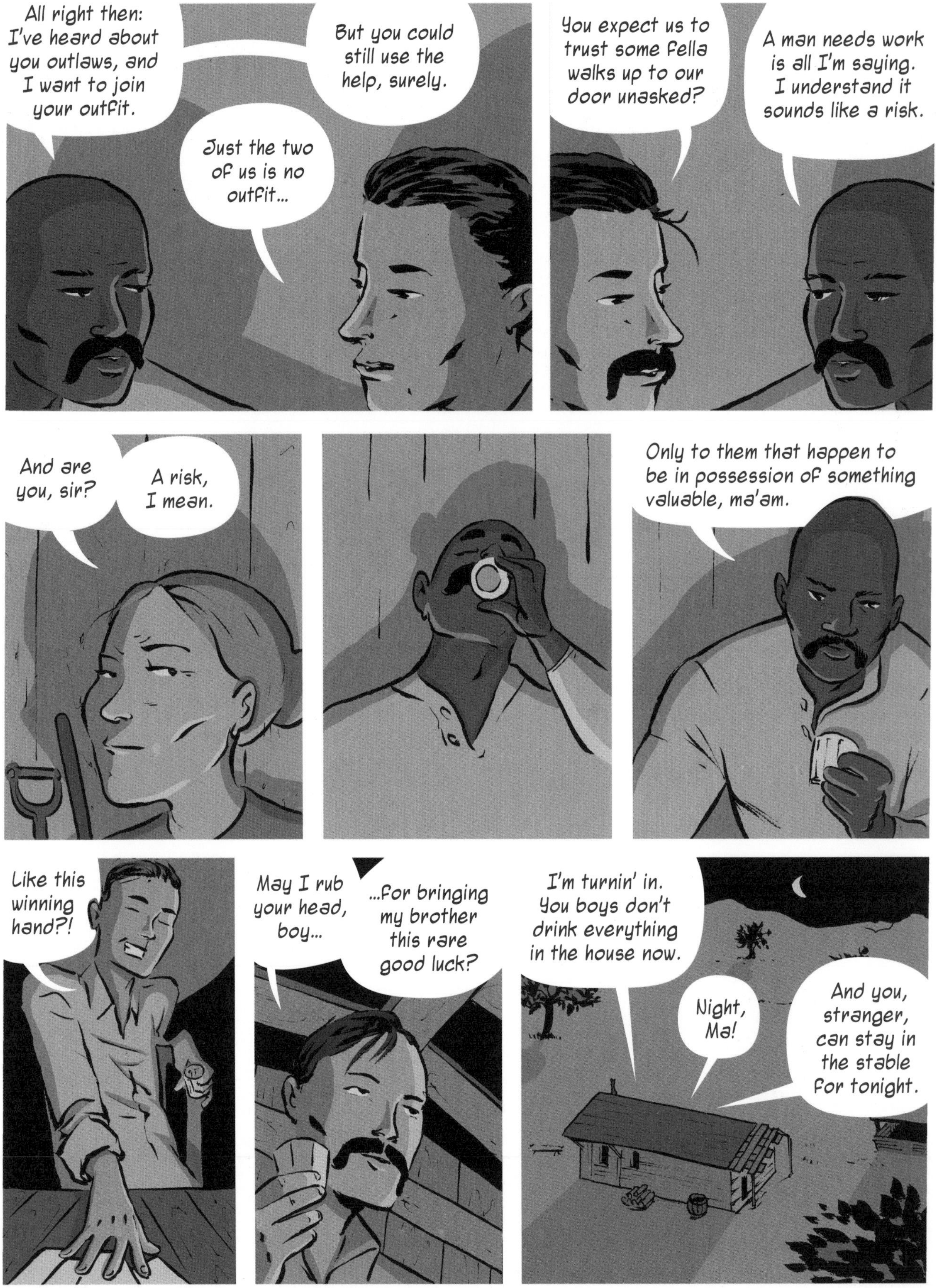
All right then: I've heard about you outlaws, and I want to join your outfit.
But you could still use the help, surely.
Just the two of us is no outfit...
You expect us to trust some fella walks up to our door unasked?
A man needs work is all I'm saying. I understand it sounds like a risk.
And are you, sir?
A risk, I mean.
Only to them that happen to be in possession of something valuable, ma'am.
Like this winning hand?!
May I rub your head, boy...
...for bringing my brother this rare good luck?
I'm turnin' in. You boys don't drink everything in the house now.
Night, Ma!
And you, stranger, can stay in the stable for tonight.

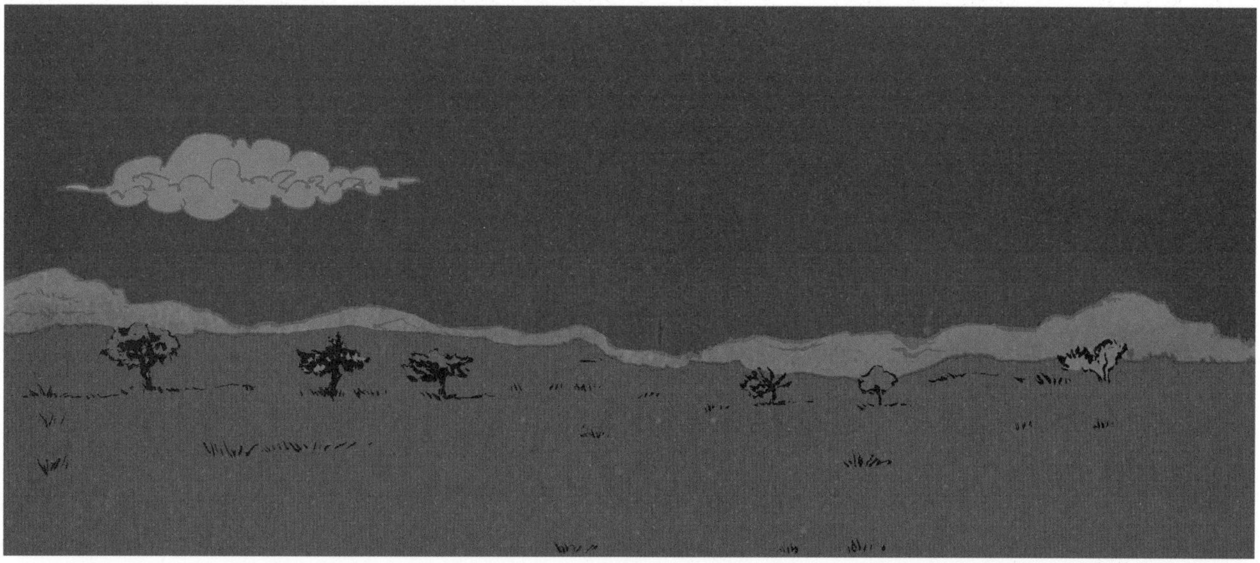
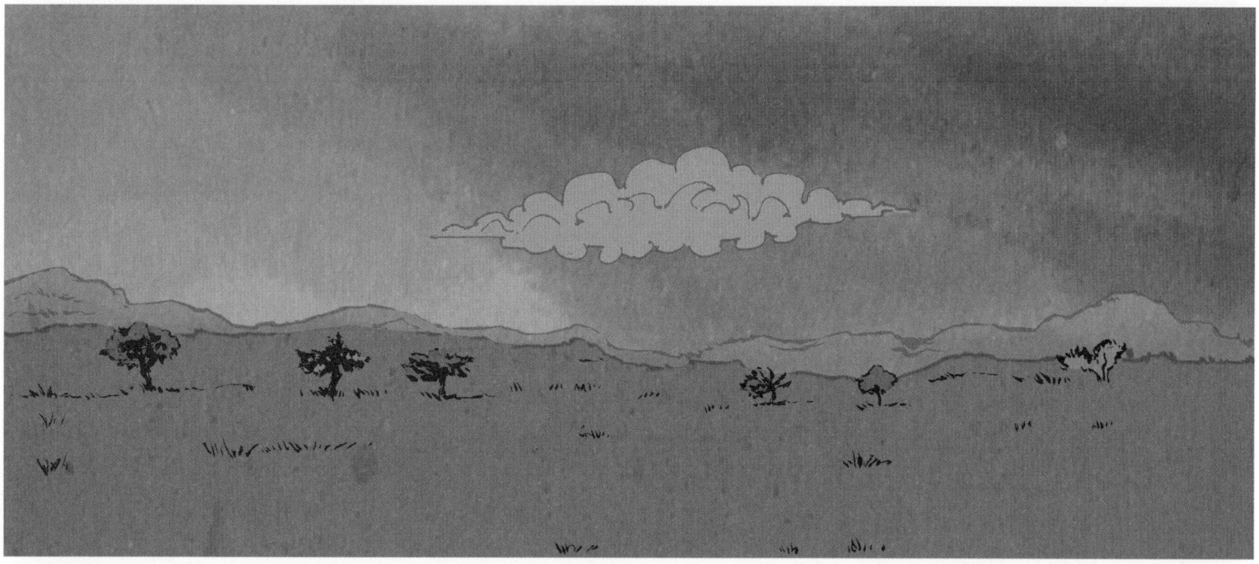
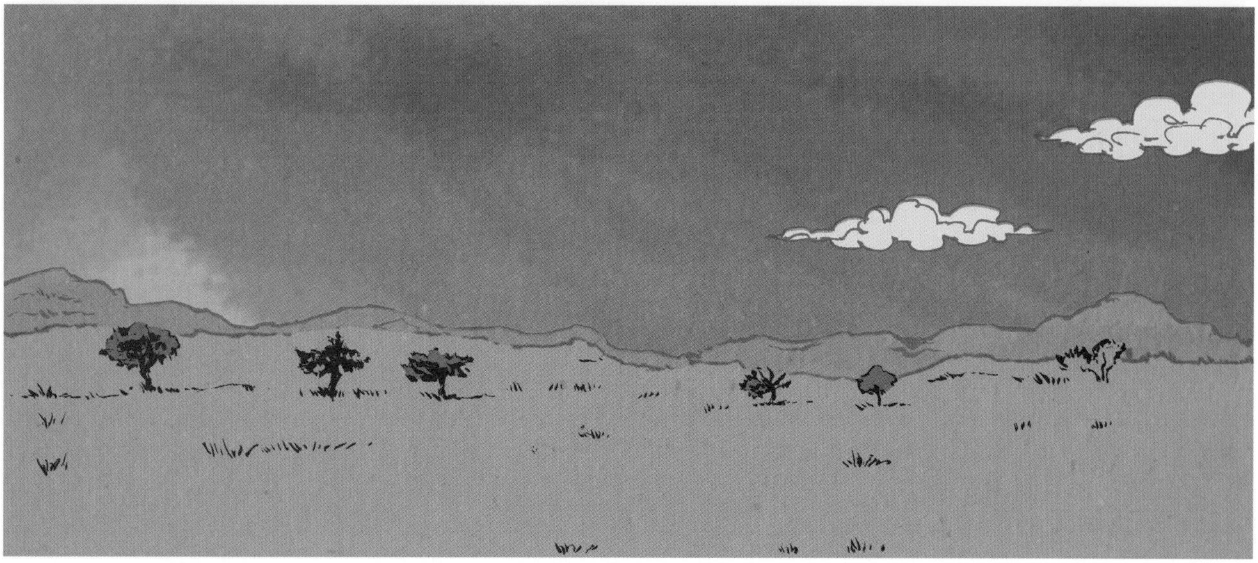

UNITED STATES OF AMERICA
US
HAL

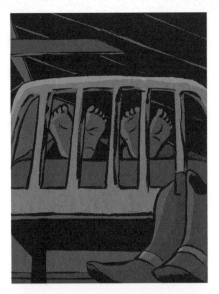

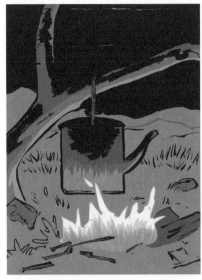

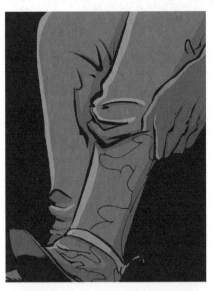

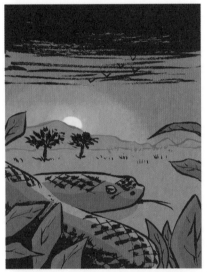

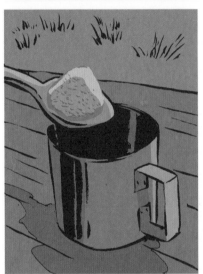

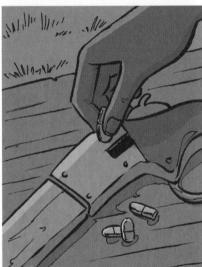

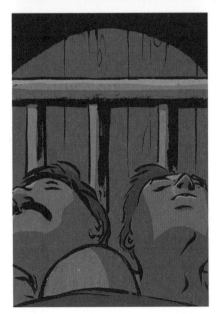

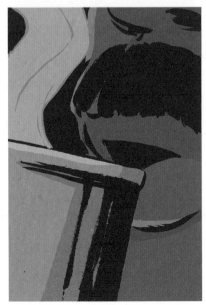

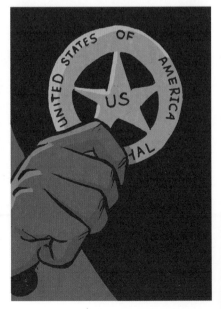

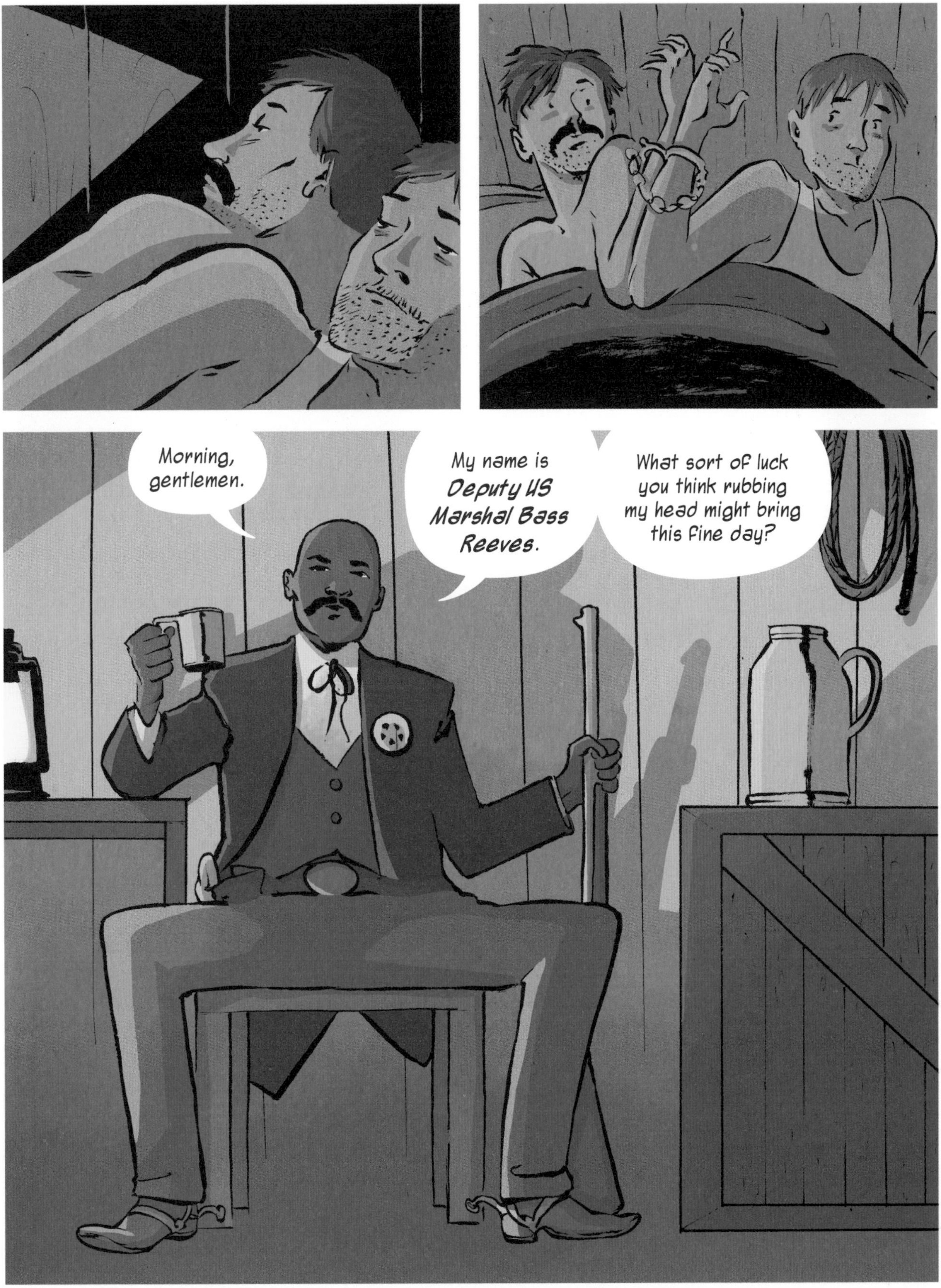
Morning, gentlemen.
My name is *Deputy US Marshal Bass Reeves.*
What sort of luck you think rubbing my head might bring this fine day?

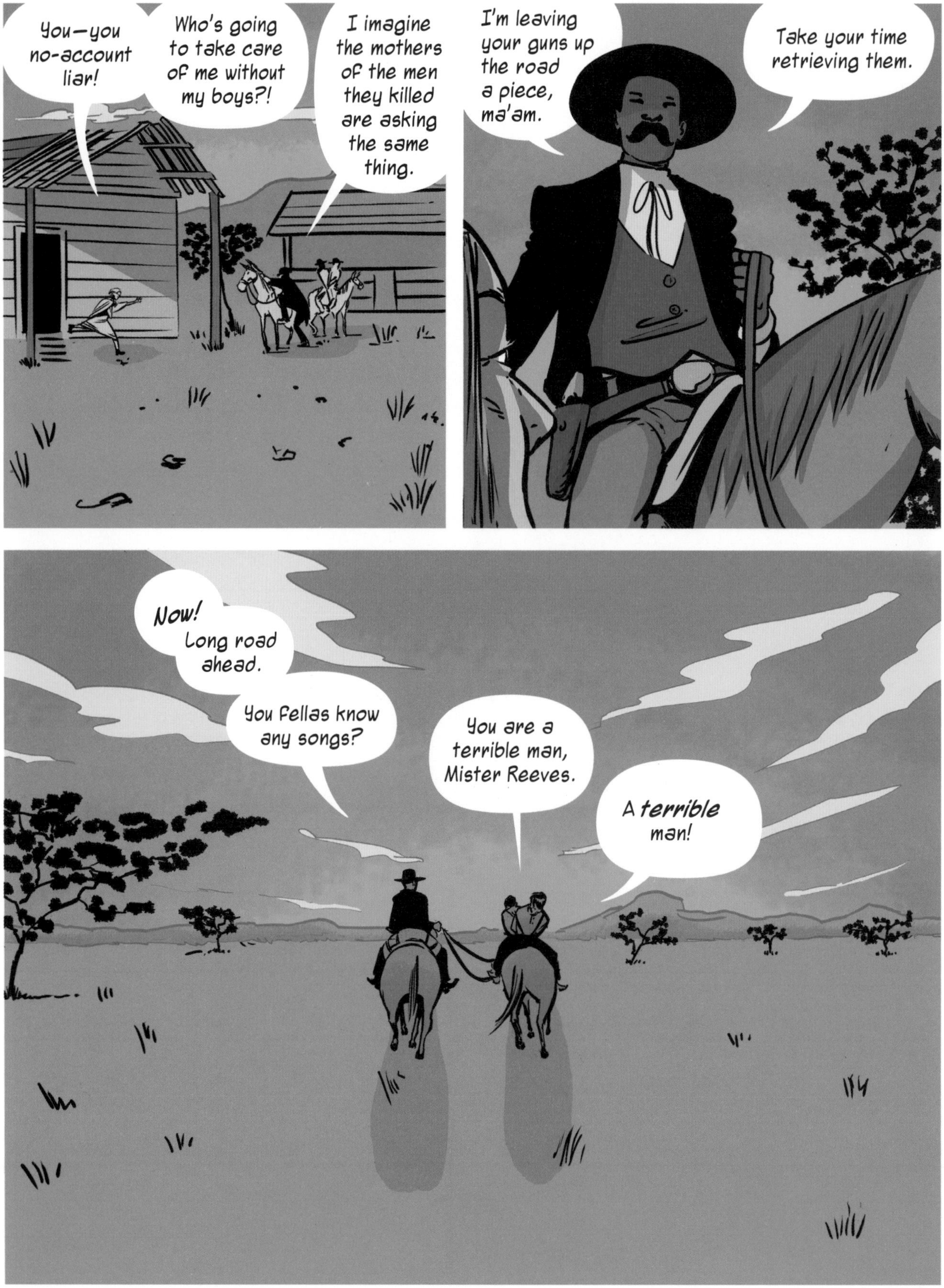

You—you no-account liar!
Who's going to take care of me without my boys?!
I imagine the mothers of the men they killed are asking the same thing.
I'm leaving your guns up the road a piece, ma'am.
Take your time retrieving them.
Now! Long road ahead.
You fellas know any songs?
You are a terrible man, Mister Reeves.
A *terrible* man!

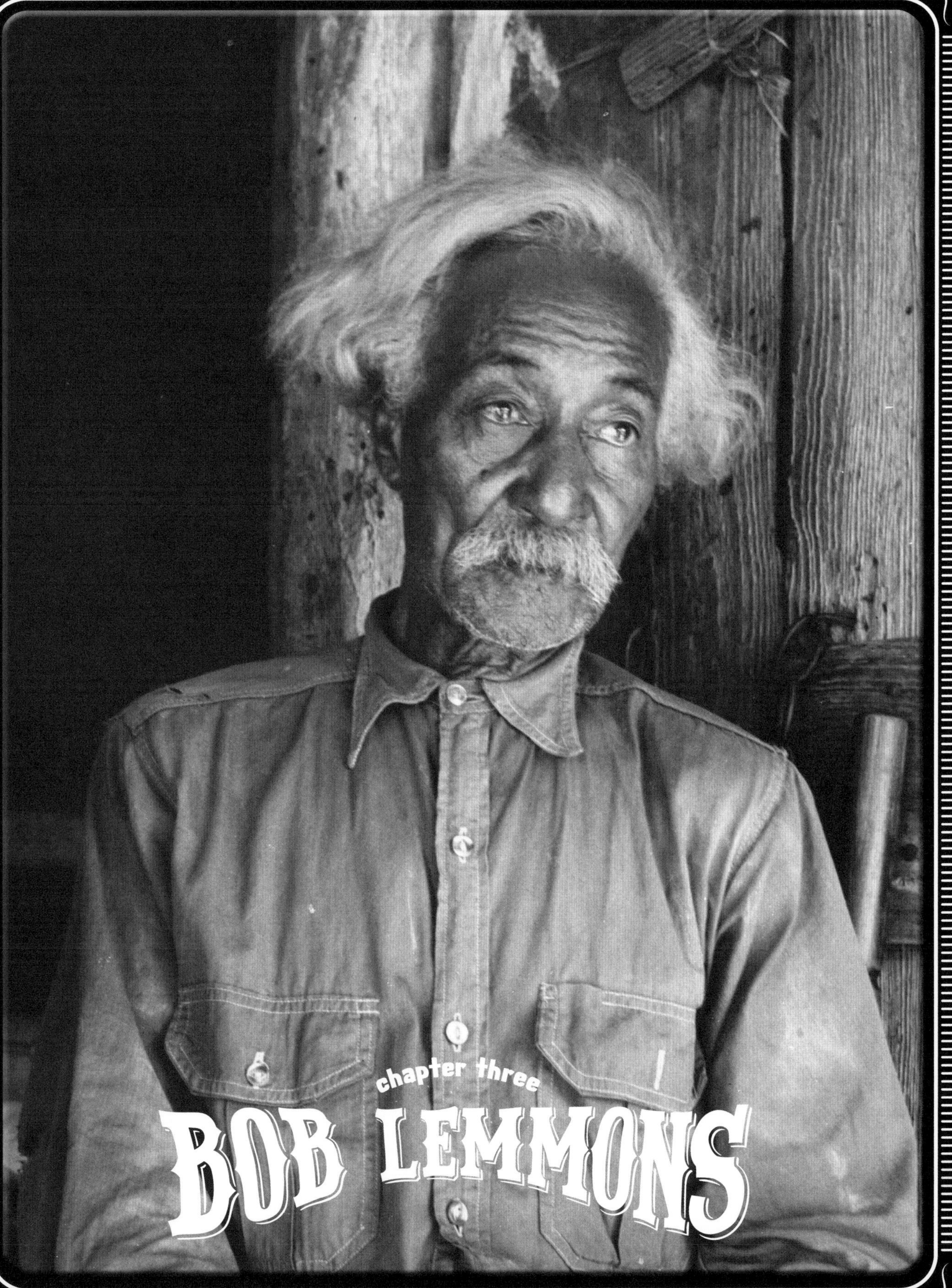

chapter three

BOB LEMMONS

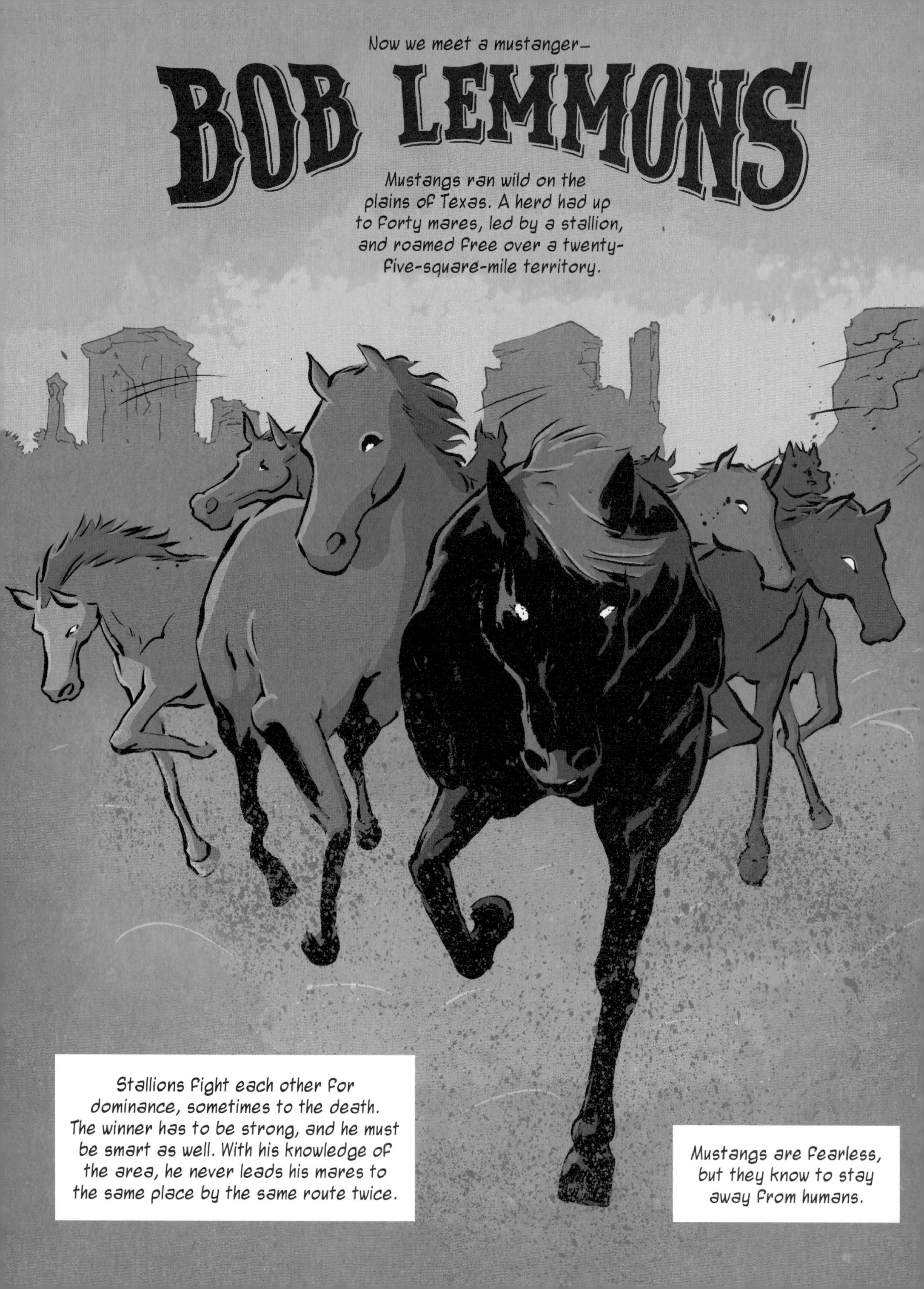
Now we meet a mustanger—
BOB LEMMONS
Mustangs ran wild on the plains of Texas. A herd had up to forty mares, led by a stallion, and roamed free over a twenty-five-square-mile territory.
Stallions fight each other for dominance, sometimes to the death. The winner has to be strong, and he must be smart as well. With his knowledge of the area, he never leads his mares to the same place by the same route twice.
Mustangs are fearless, but they know to stay away from humans.

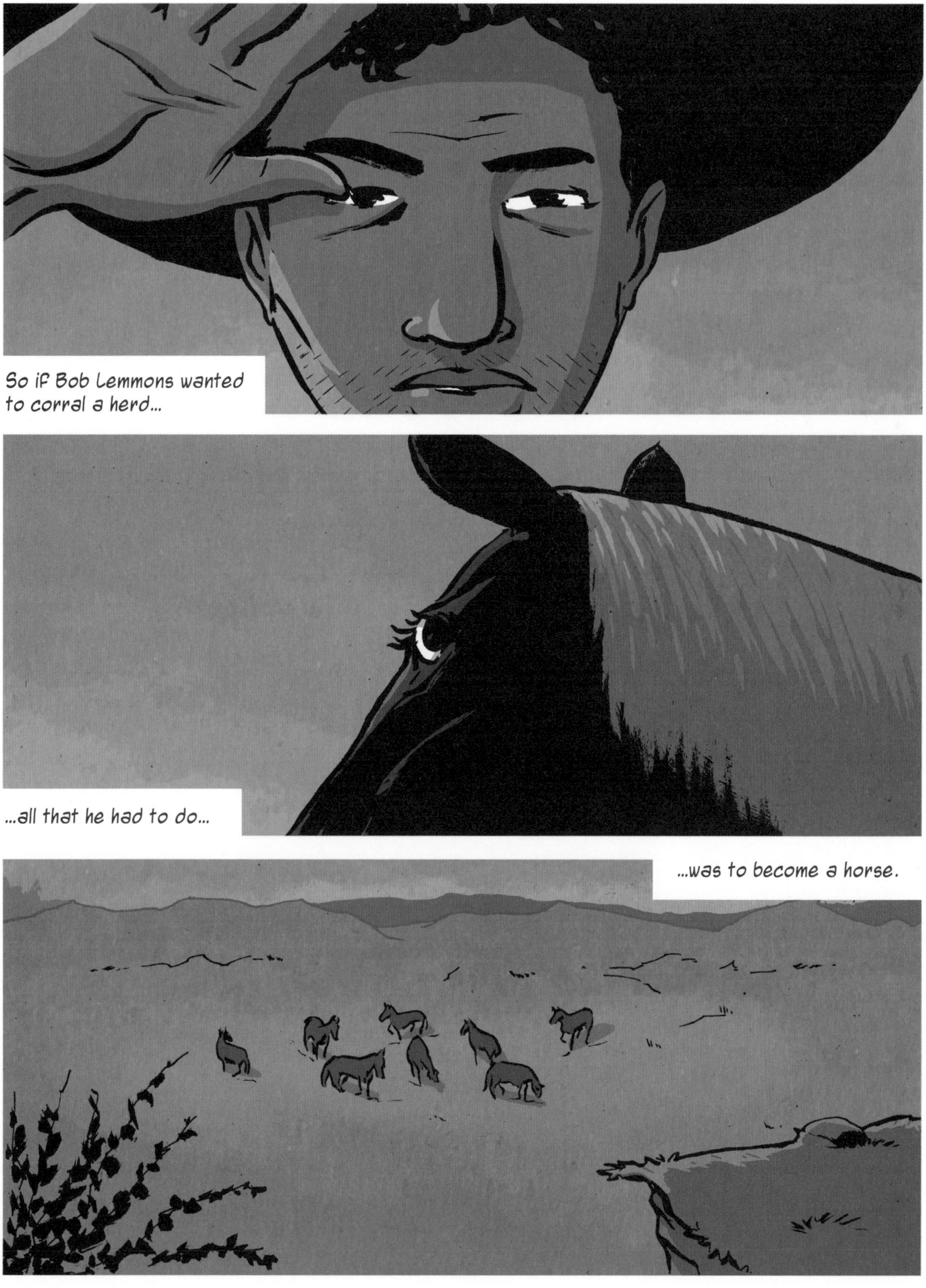
So if Bob Lemmons wanted to corral a herd...
...all that he had to do...
...was to become a horse.

Other mustangers worked in teams, trying to surround the herd. Most often, they killed the stallion, then "walked" the leaderless mares for two weeks or more. Only then could the starved and worn-out horses be roped and brought in. Sometimes the mustanger's own horse would even die of exhaustion.

Bob knew that wasn't right.

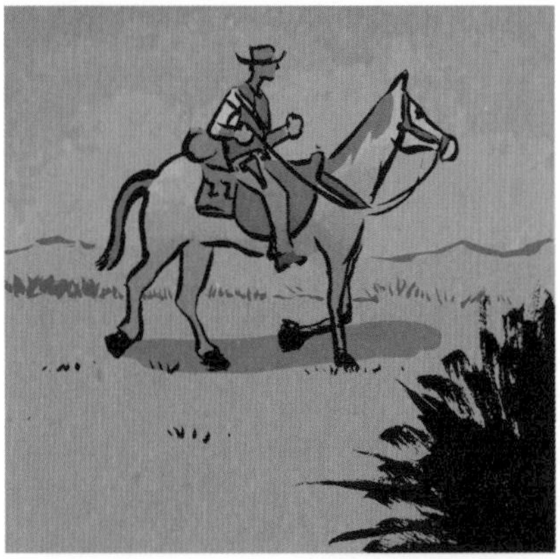

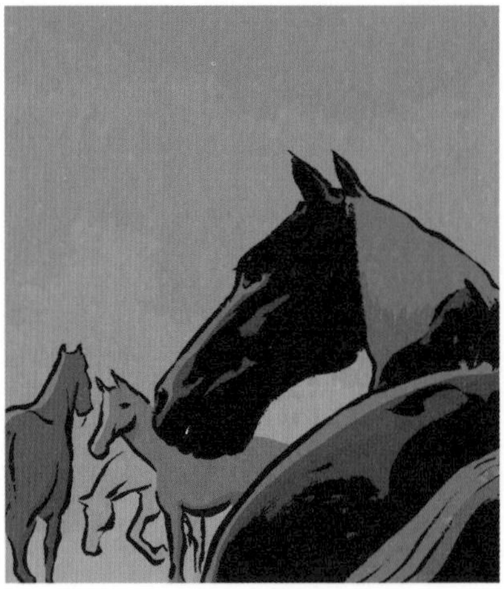

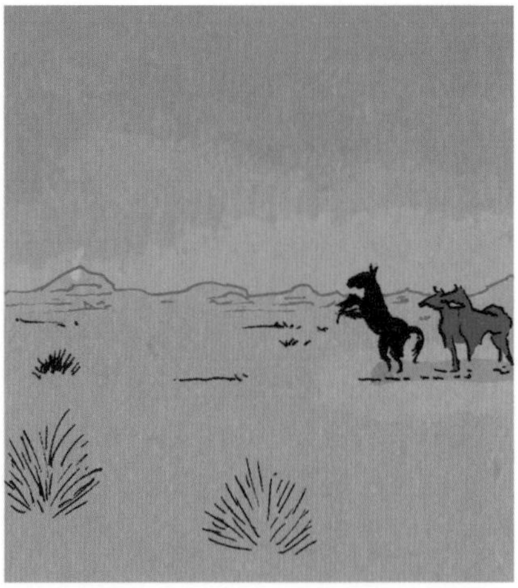

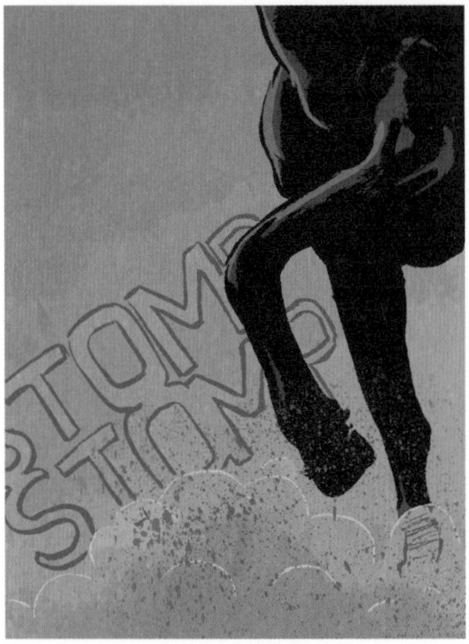
STOMP
STOMP

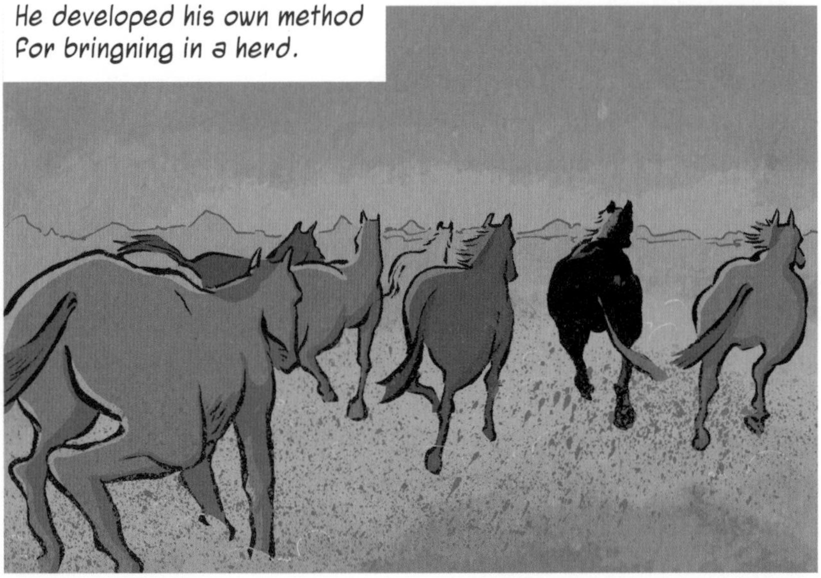
He developed his own method for bringning in a herd.

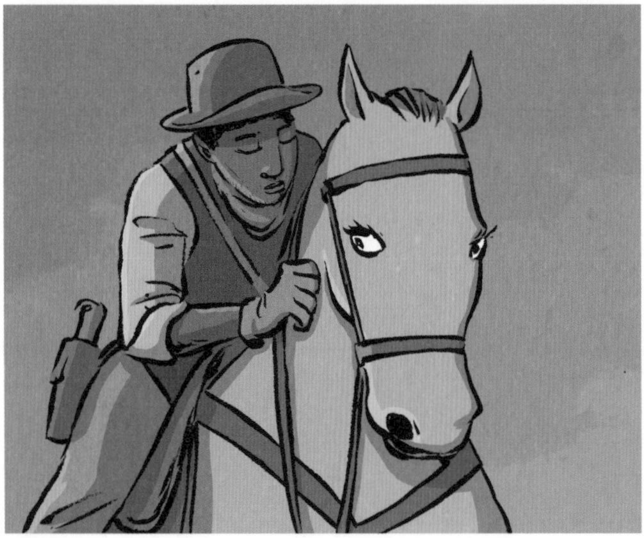

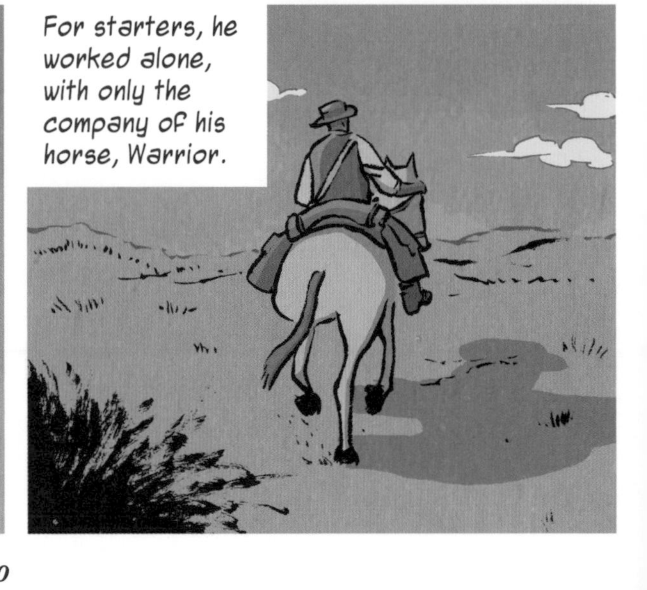
For starters, he worked alone, with only the company of his horse, Warrior.

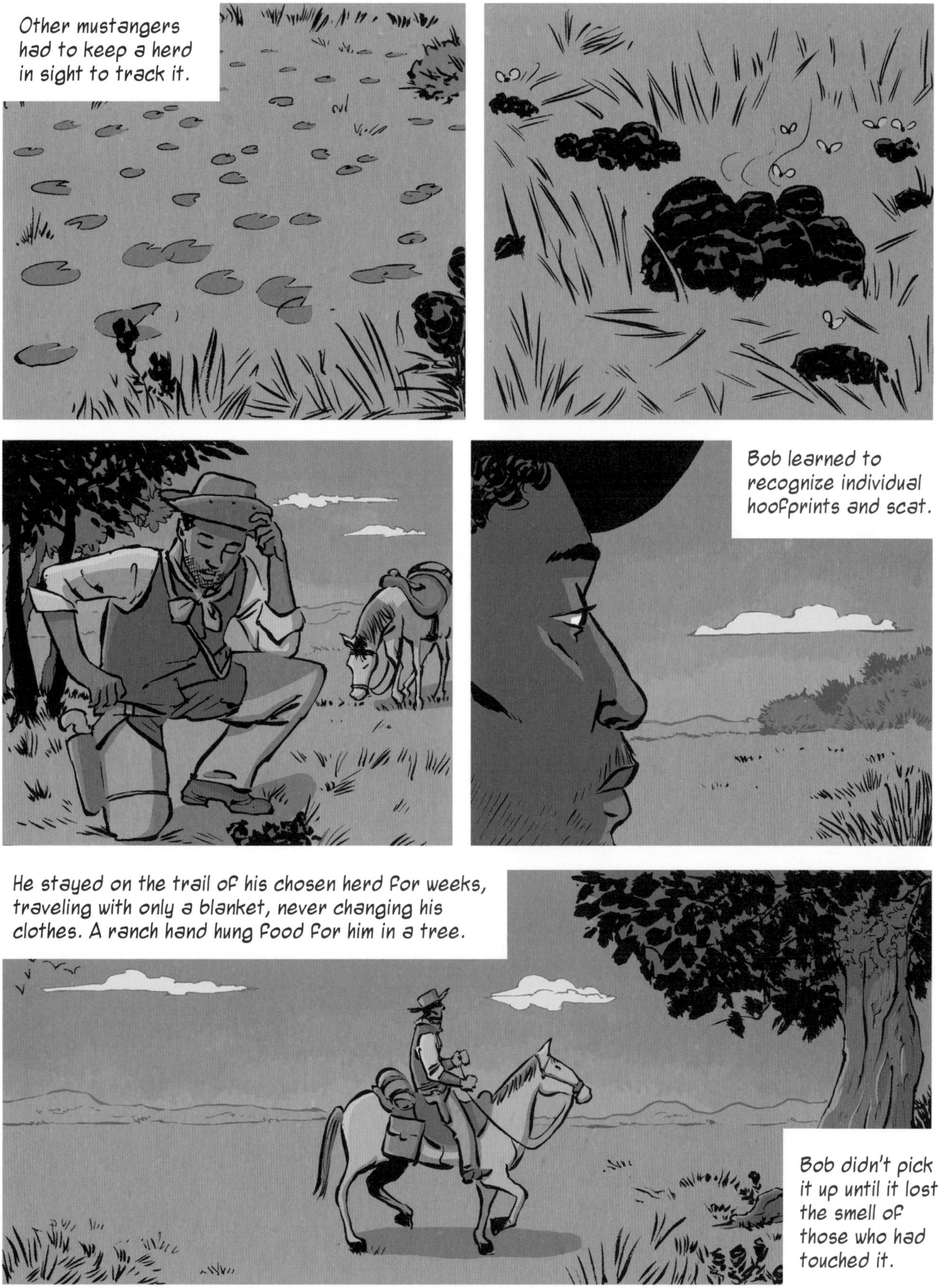
Other mustangers had to keep a herd in sight to track it.
Bob learned to recognize individual hoofprints and scat.
He stayed on the trail of his chosen herd for weeks, traveling with only a blanket, never changing his clothes. A ranch hand hung food for him in a tree.
Bob didn't pick it up until it lost the smell of those who had touched it.

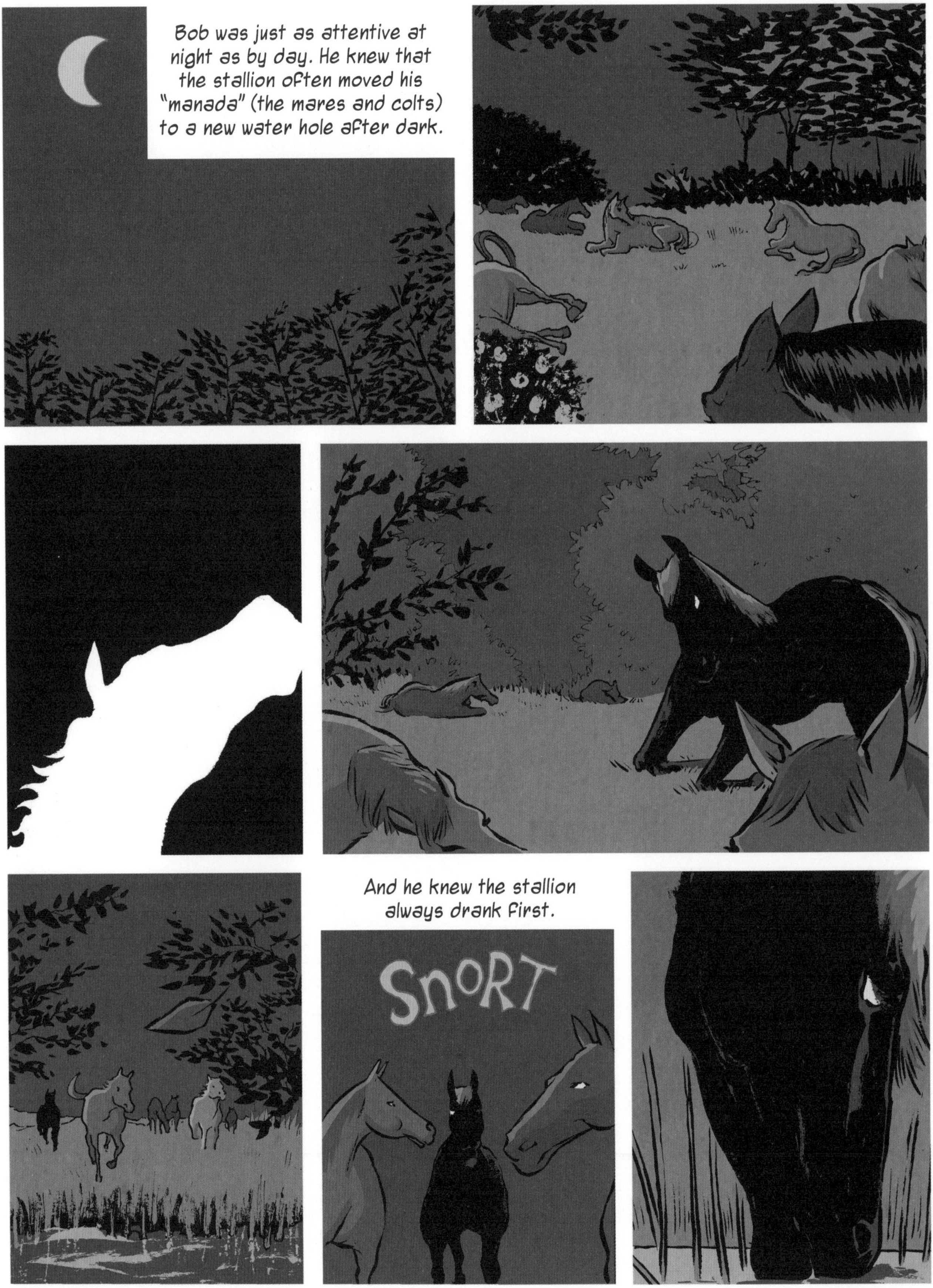
Bob was just as attentive at night as by day. He knew that the stallion often moved his "manada" (the mares and colts) to a new water hole after dark.
And he knew the stallion always drank first.
SNORT

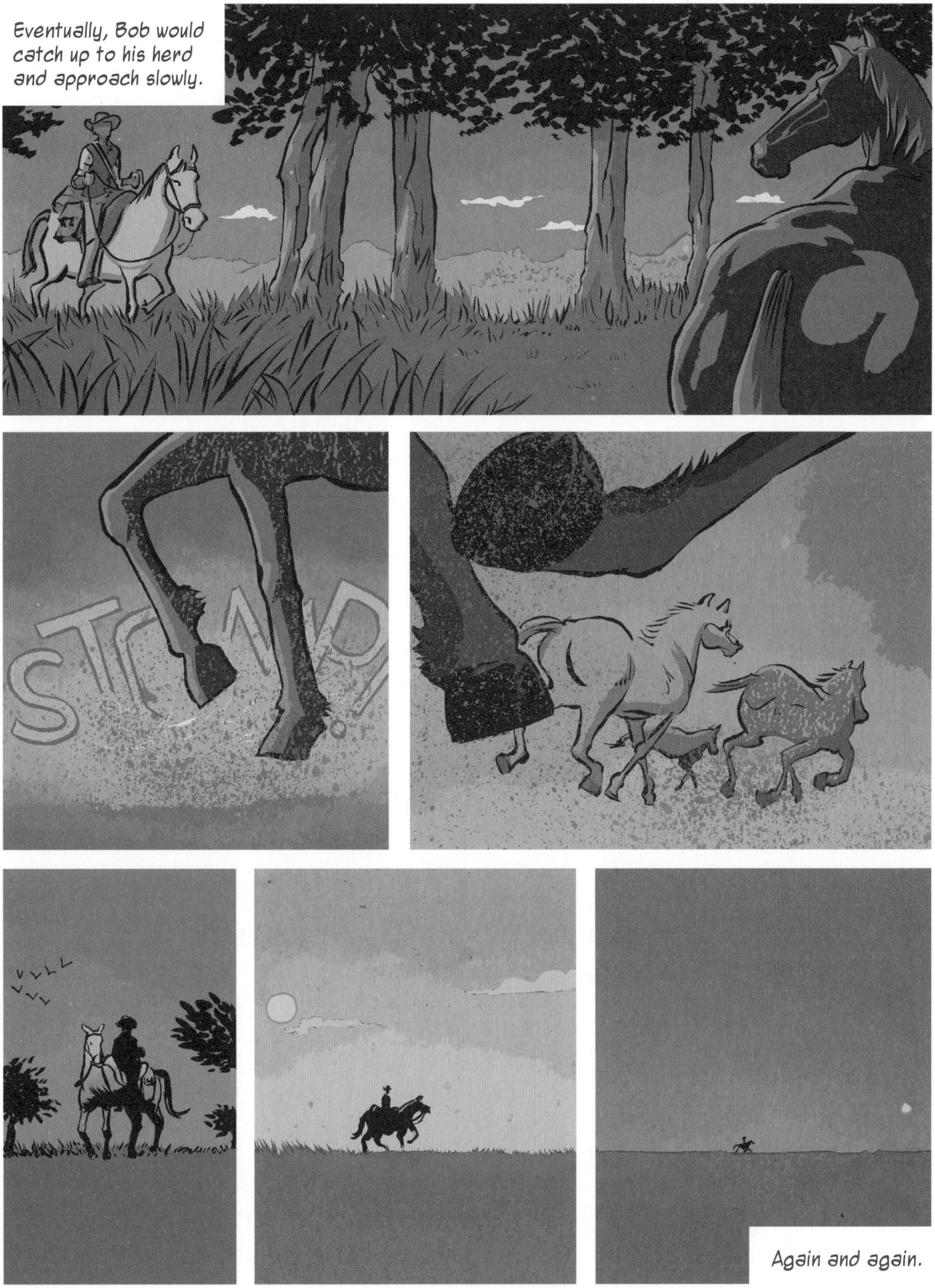
Eventually, Bob would catch up to his herd and approach slowly.
STOMP!
Again and again.

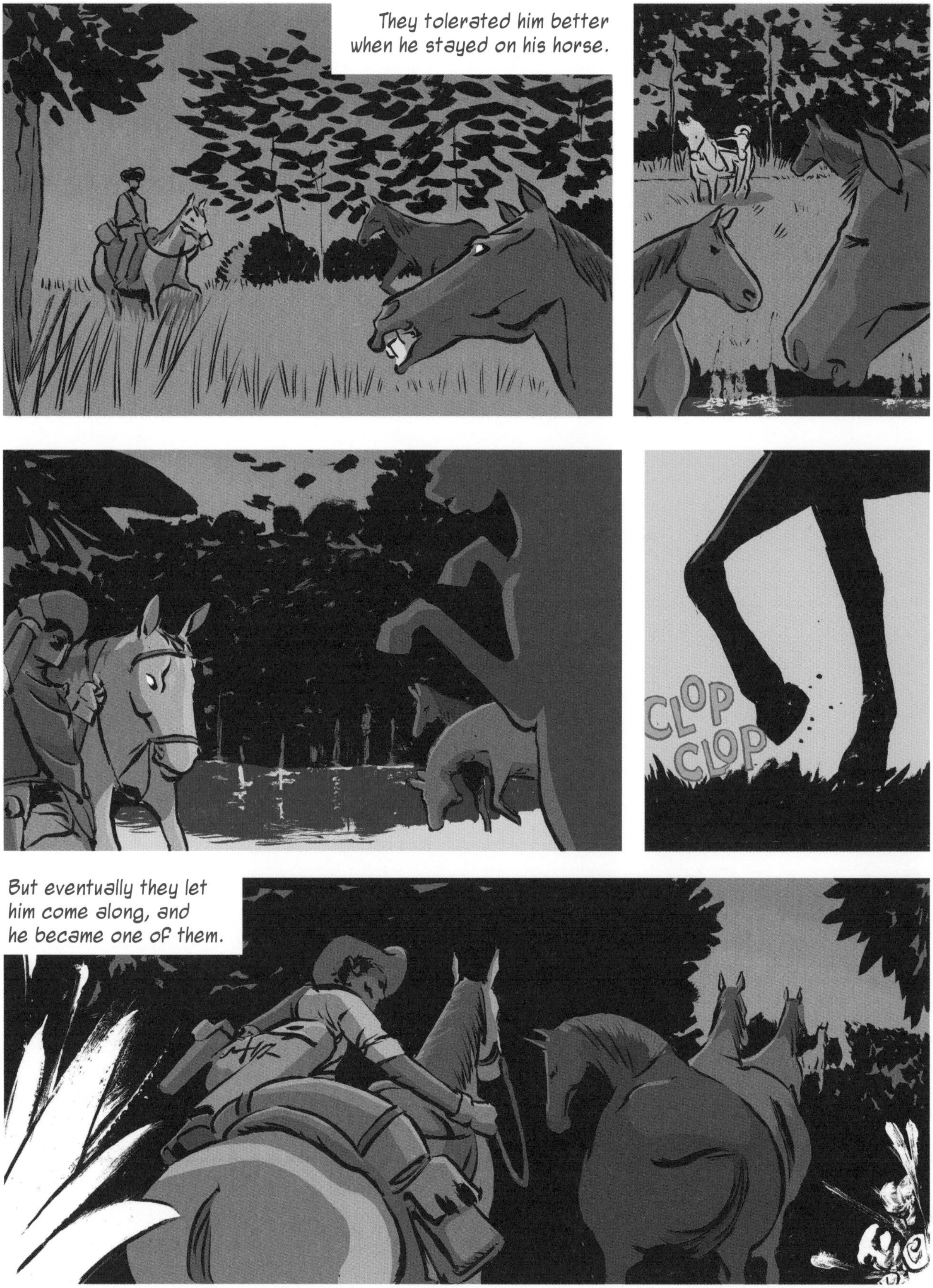
They tolerated him better when he stayed on his horse.
CLOP CLOP
But eventually they let him come along, and he became one of them.

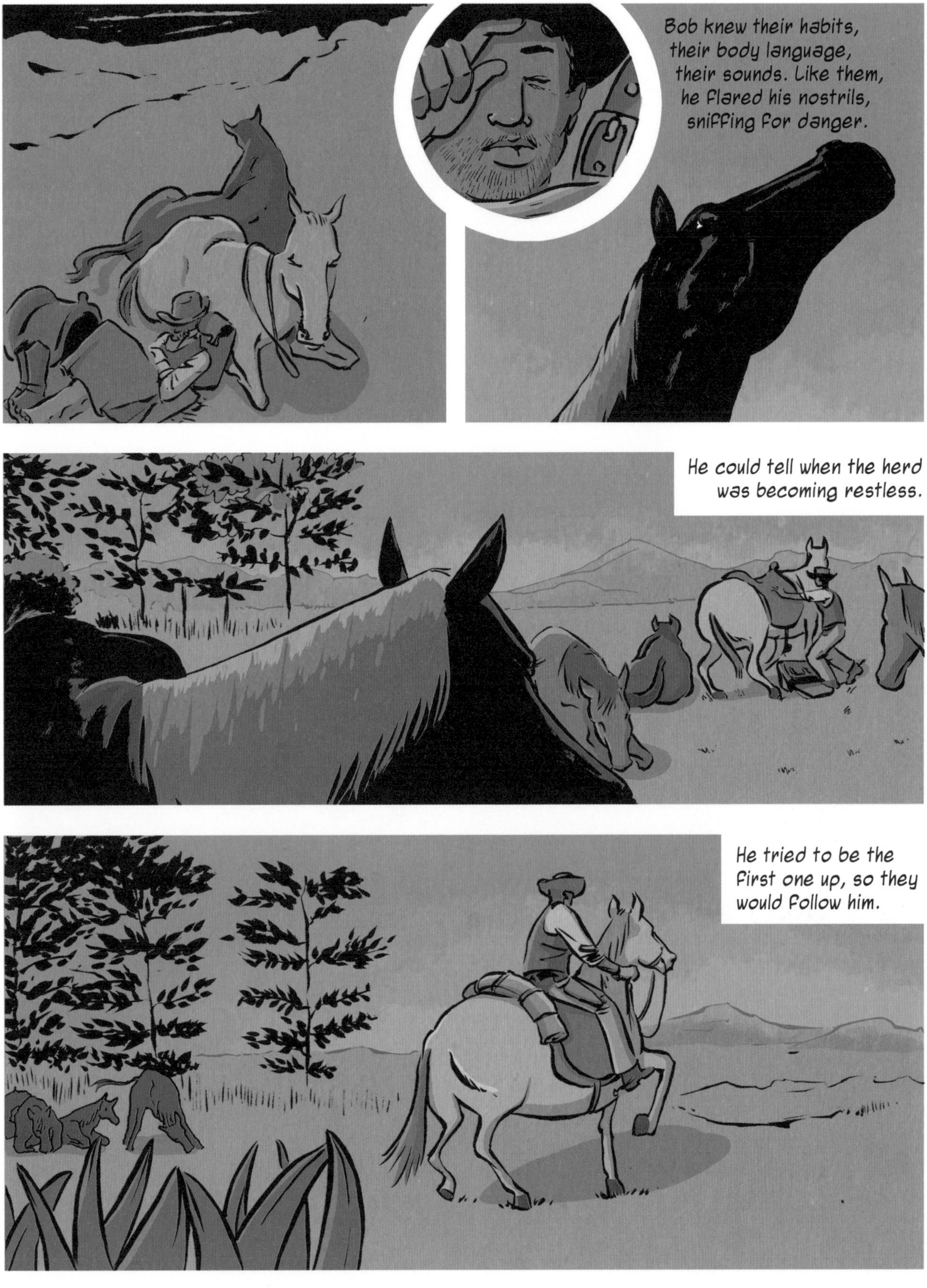
Bob knew their habits, their body language, their sounds. Like them, he flared his nostrils, sniffing for danger.
He could tell when the herd was becoming restless.
He tried to be the first one up, so they would follow him.

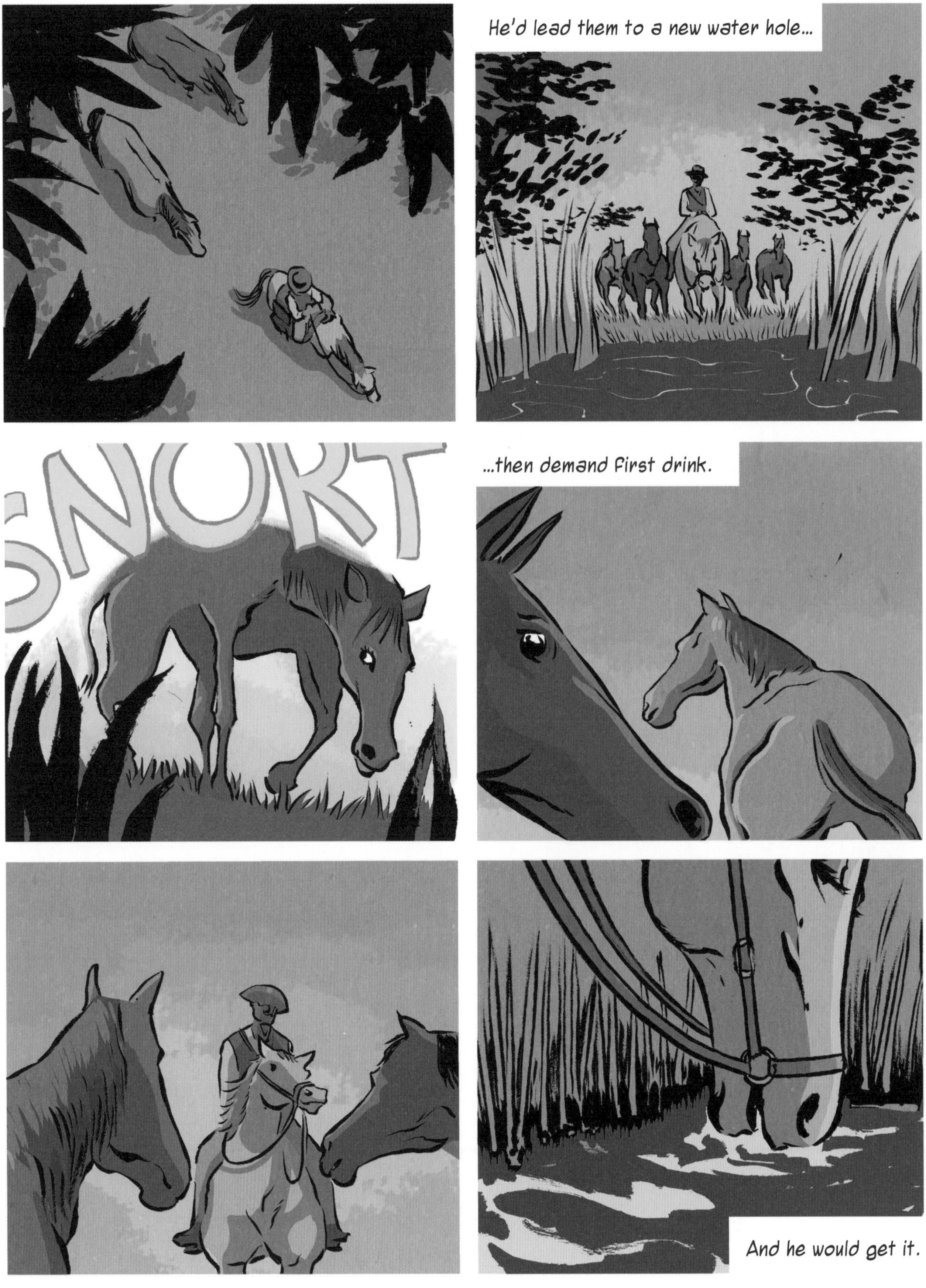
He'd lead them to a new water hole...
SNORT
...then demand first drink.
And he would get it.

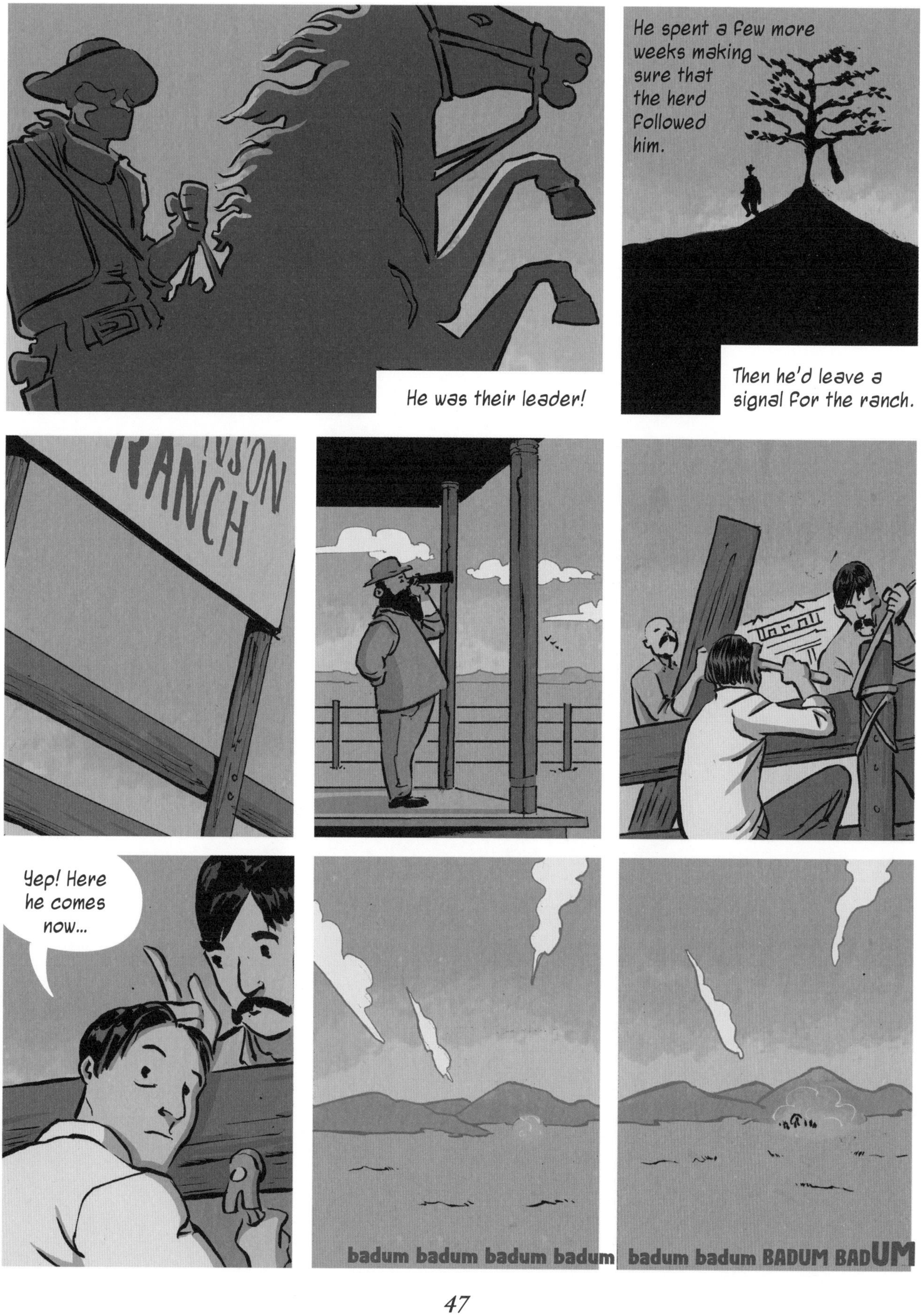
He was their leader!
He spent a few more weeks making sure that the herd followed him.
Then he'd leave a signal for the ranch.
RANCH
Yep! Here he comes now...
badum badum badum badum
badum badum BADUM BADUM

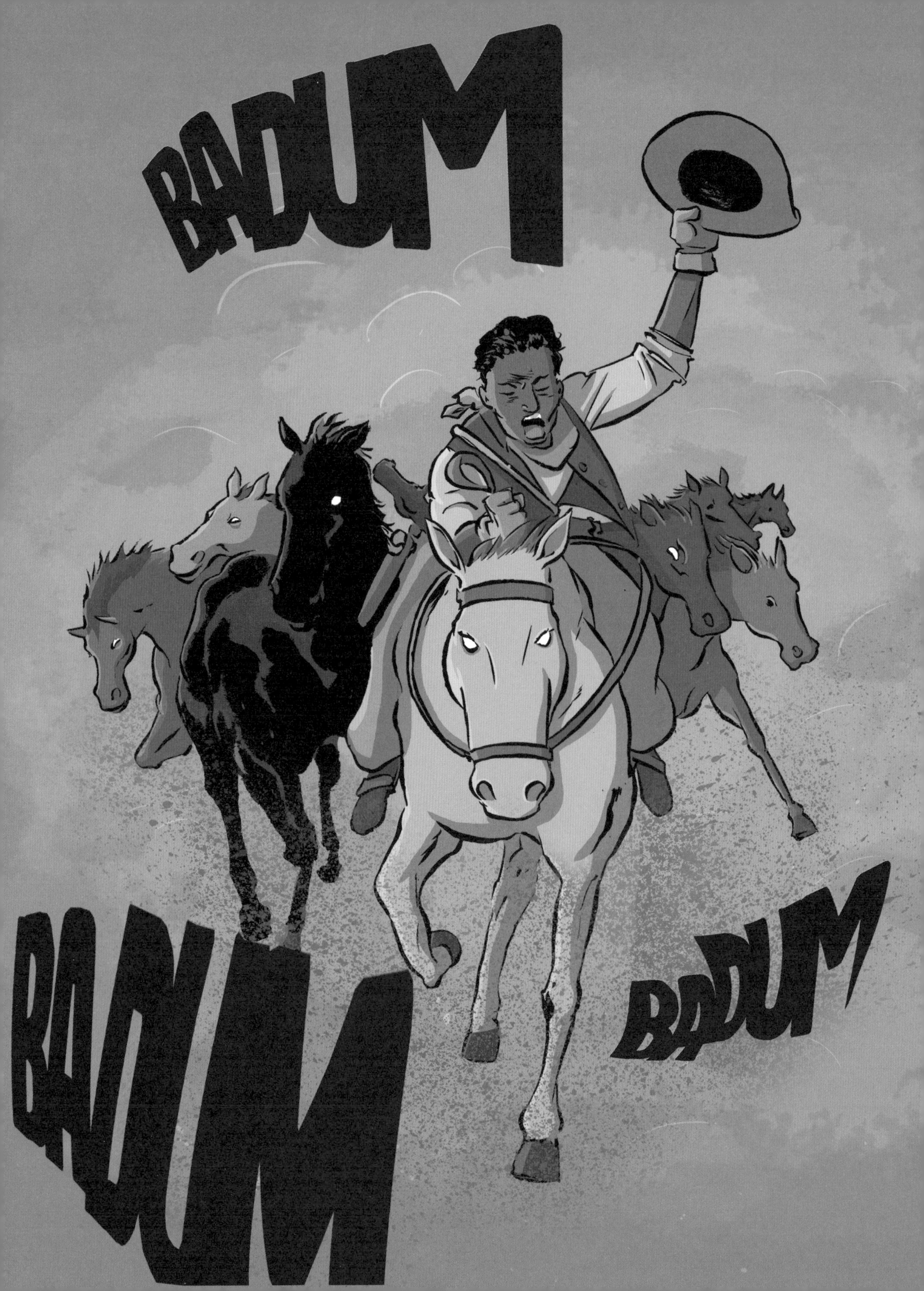
BADUM
BADUM
BADUM

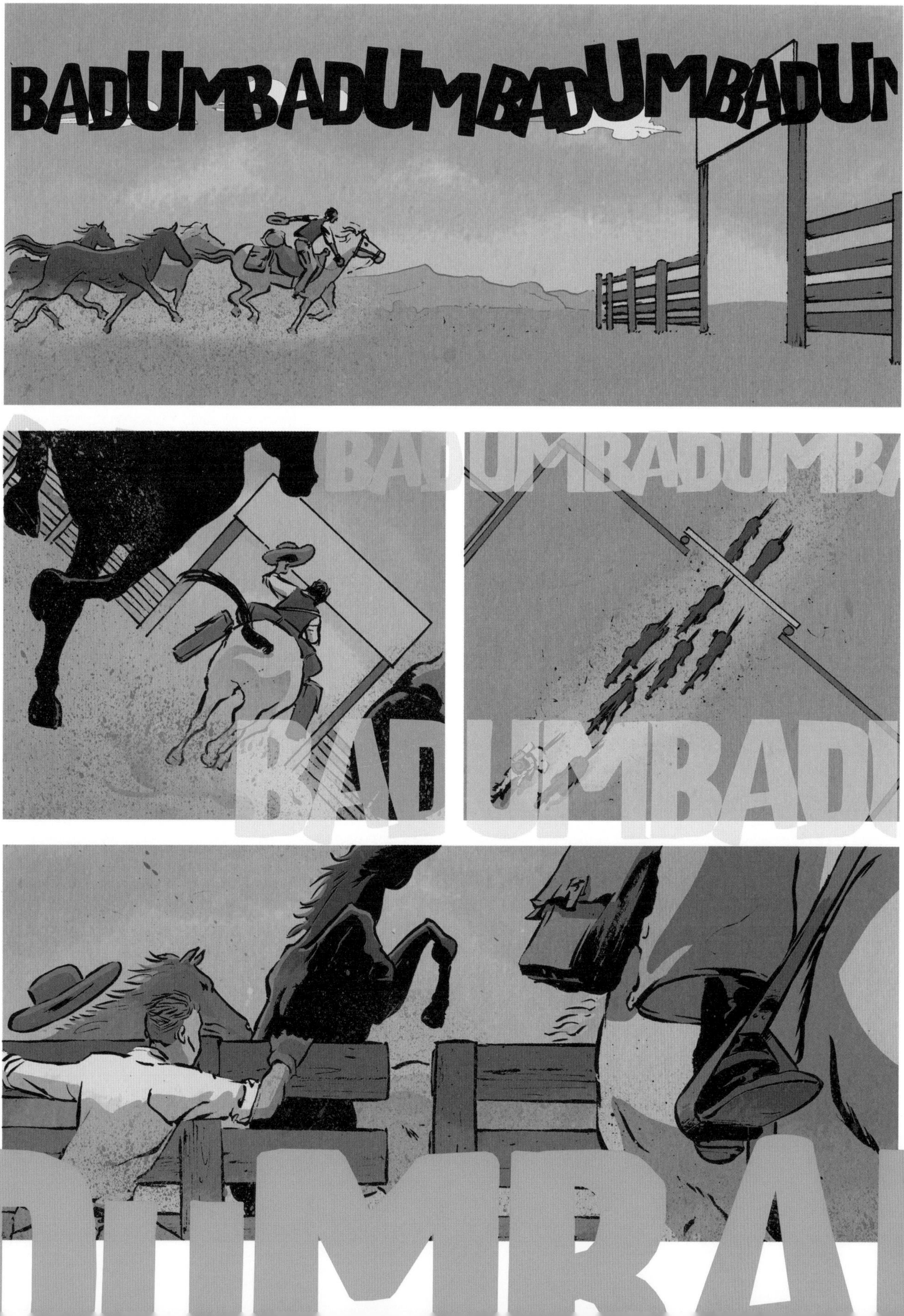
BADUMBADUMBADUMBADU
BADUMBADUMB
BADUMBAD

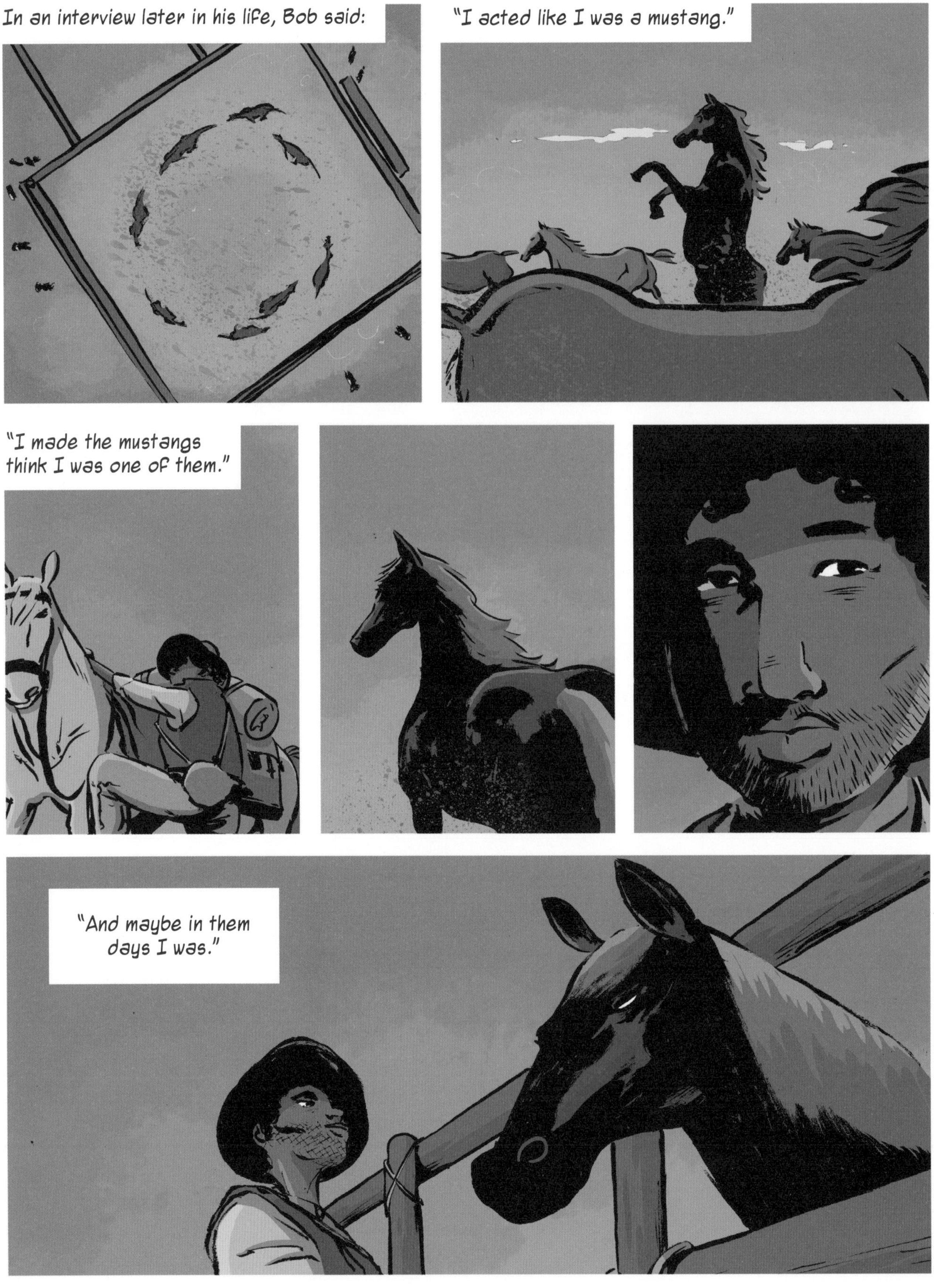
In an interview later in his life, Bob said:
"I acted like I was a mustang."
"I made the mustangs think I was one of them."
"And maybe in them days I was."

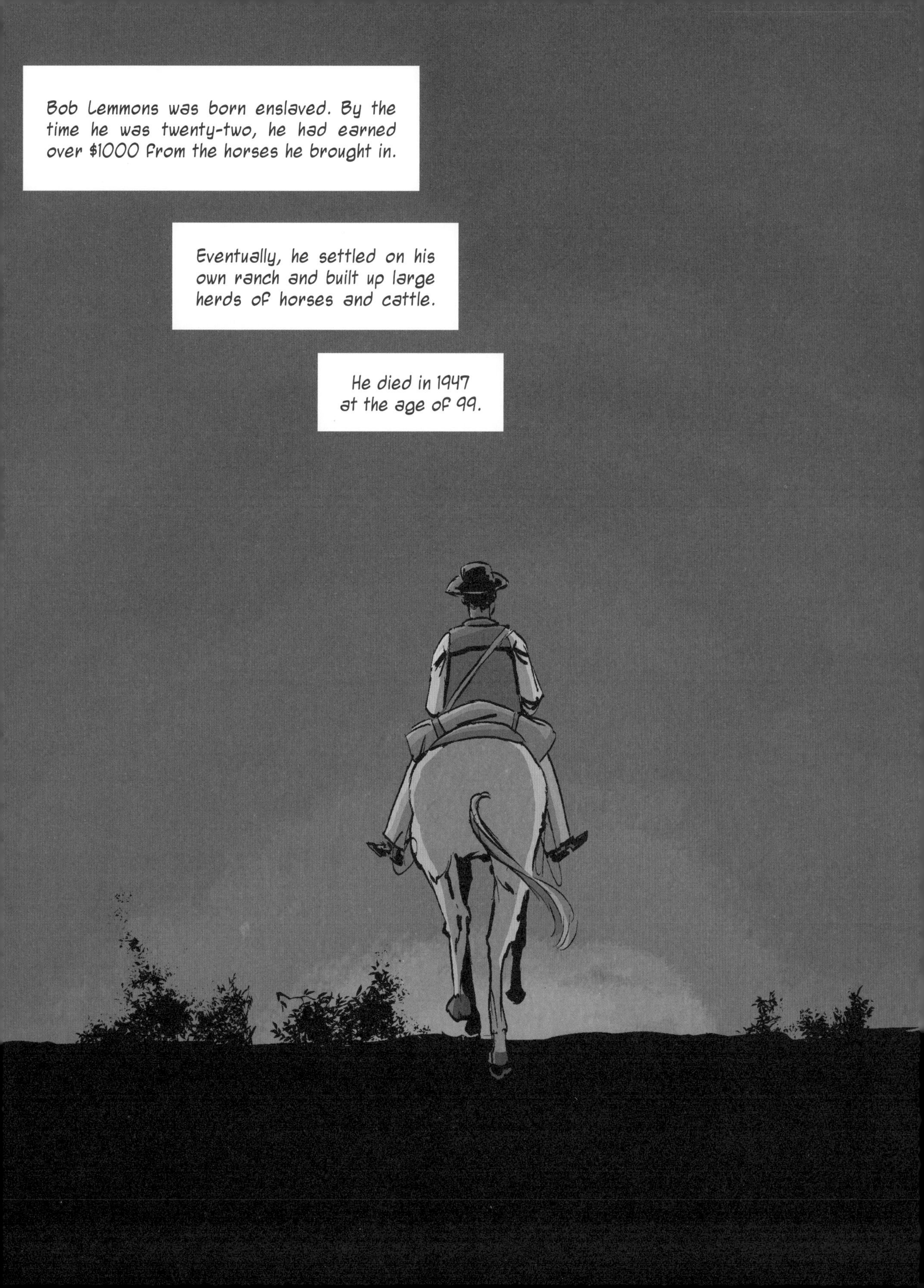
Bob Lemmons was born enslaved. By the time he was twenty-two, he had earned over $1000 from the horses he brought in.
Eventually, he settled on his own ranch and built up large herds of horses and cattle.
He died in 1947 at the age of 99.

ABOUT THE AUTHORS

JAMES OTIS SMITH is a writer and artist living in Brooklyn. He has collaborated on several graphic novels, including *Showtime at the Apollo*. *Black Heroes of the Wild West* is his first book as author and illustrator. He says: "I was interested in finding stories of ordinary people who lived during Reconstruction, the period between the Civil War and the era of anti-Black terrorism called Jim Crow. This was the first time Black people in America were able to choose where they wanted to live, work, and raise their families. It was also the first time they could choose their own names. America was still deciding what kind of country it wanted to become, and these newly freed people—still a few decades shy of being full citizens—were in the process of becoming as well. These three stories are not the typical tales of violence in the Old West, but those of everyday African Americans born into slavery who had the courage and strength to choose to be whoever they wanted to be."

KADIR NELSON *(Introduction)* is an accomplished painter, illustrator, and children's book author. He has contributed many memorable covers for *The New Yorker* (such as the "Eustace Negro" painting for the 90th Anniversary of the magazine shown here).

His paintings are in the private and public permanent collections of several notable institutions including the Muskegon Museum of Art, the National Baseball Hall of Fame, the International Olympic Committee, and the US House of Representatives. He has painted album covers for Michael Jackson and for Drake. He is the author or the illustrator of more than thirty children's books including *The Undefeated*, written by Kwame Alexander, which received the Caldecott Medal, the Coretta Scott King Award, and a Newbery Honor.

WHO WERE THE REAL COWBOYS?

The cowboy lifestyle has been glamorized in Westerns—books, movies, or television shows—but cowboys were actually poor young men who owned little more than their horses. They wore large hats with wide brims to shield themselves from the sun and bandannas to cover their noses when riding in the clouds of dust raised by cattle. And they were much more diverse than the Hollywood stereotype suggests. Many were Mexican, mestizo, African American, or Native American.

NYPL Digital Collection - George Arents Collection

Round the World With Cracklin' Jane/Maine Public Radio

"An Ostoho Cow Boy", Apache tribe, 1903, by Edward S. Curtis. Library of Congress

COWBOYS: MEXICAN ORIGINS

Hundreds of different groups of native peoples lived in the West for at least 11,000 years before the arrival of Europeans in the 1500s. Spaniards brought in cattle and horses and trained Native Americans to ride and herd. Cowhands were known as *vaqueros* (from *vaca*, the Spanish for cow). When Mexico won its independence from Spain in 1821, its territory included a large part of what is now the US. By the end of the Mexican-American War (1846-48,) it had lost half its territory. White settlers were encouraged to move in with promises of free land and tax breaks. In the first census of Texas as a US state in 1860, African American slaves accounted for almost a third of the settler population. The Civil War (1861-65) sent white Texans to fight in the East, leaving slaves to hone their skills tending the land and cattle herds. When European newcomers arrived in the West, they adopted the *vaquero* style. *Vaquero* is the root word for the English term "buckaroo." As a matter of fact, much of the vocabulary used by cowboys is derived from the Spanish: a *sombrero* is literally a shade-maker; "cinch" comes from *cincha*, a strap used to saddle horses; cowboy "chaps" come from the word *chaparro*, a short and stocky person; "lariat" comes from *reata*, a braided rawhide rope;"lasso" comes from *lazo*, a knot; and bronco (as in "bronco buster") is Spanish for rough and wild.

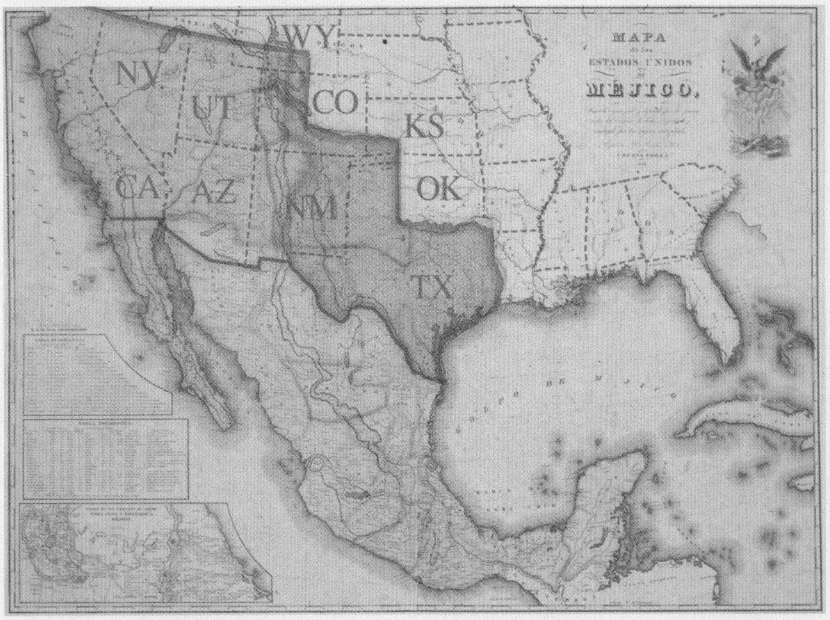

MAPA
ESTADOS UNIDOS
MÉJICO.
WY
NV
UT
CO
KS
CA
AZ
NM
OK
TX

White, Gallaher & White Mapa de los Estados Unidos de Méjico 1828

Overlaid (in green) on a map of the "United States of Mexico" from 1828 is the Mexican territory that has since become part of the USA. It includes six states: California, Nevada, Utah, Arizona, New Mexico, Texas, and parts of four others: Wyoming, Kansas, Colorado, and Oklahoma.

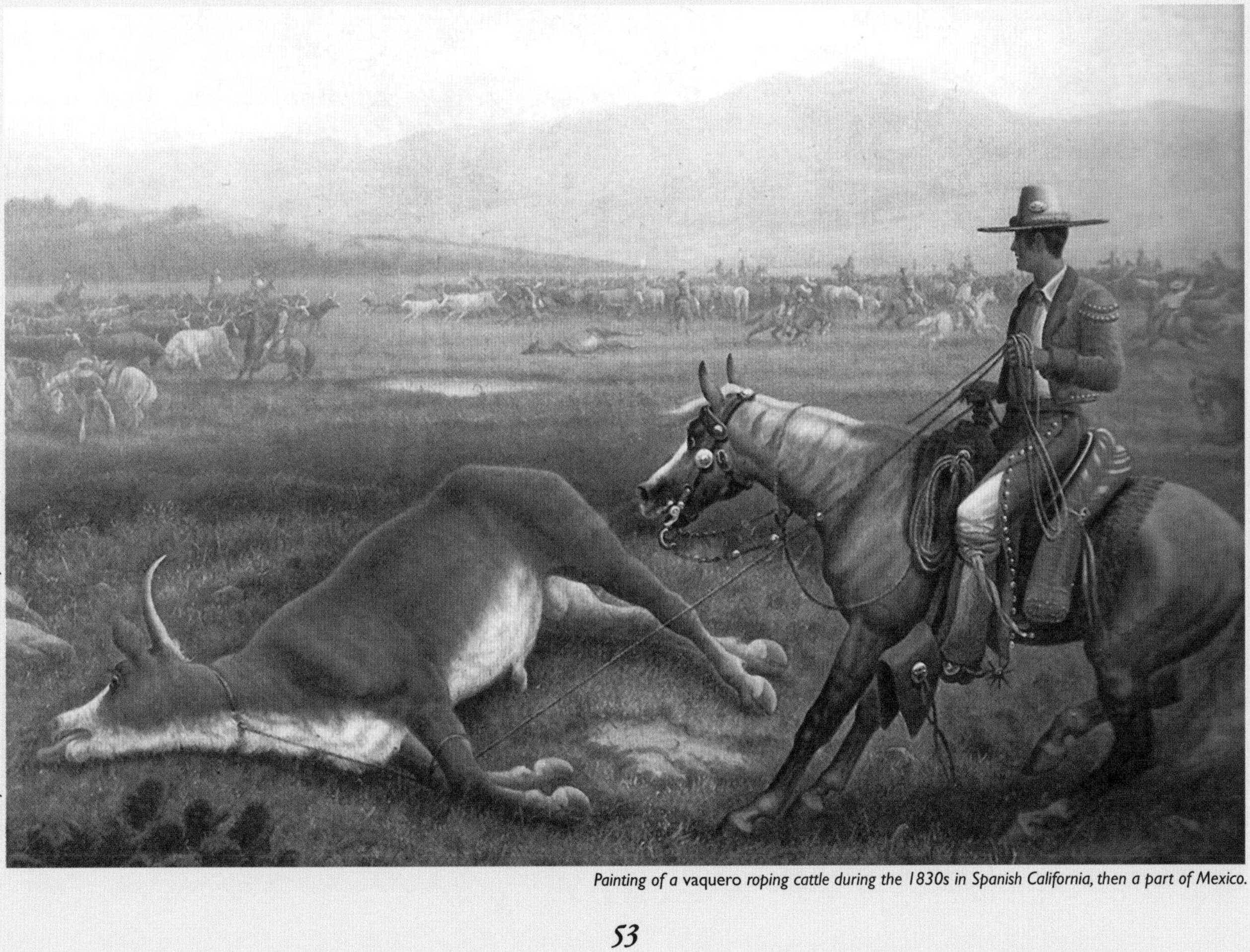

Courtesy The Old West, "The Cowboys," *Time Life Books*

Painting of a vaquero roping cattle during the 1830s in Spanish California, then a part of Mexico.

CATTLE DRIVES AND RAILROADS

The 1800s saw a relentless expansion of American and European settlers towards the Western frontier and America's encroachement on Native American territories and ancestral homesteads. Encouraged by offers of free land, American and European settlers who moved to Texas found plenty of cattle and horses roaming free–if they could catch them. The price of beef was quite low there, but fresh beef fetched much higher prices in Northern cities and the East. Starting around 1865, as railheads were established in places like Abilene, Kansas, ranchers hired cowboys to catch, brand, and then drive large herds north to bring them to market through arduous territory. A diverse crew of a dozen men herded up to 3000 cattle, covering only 15 miles a day on average–they didn't want their animals to lose weight on the journey. Each cowboy had three horses, which were looked after by a horse wrangler, usually the youngest member of the crew. The men kept the cattle calm on the drives by talking or singing to them. During storms, they took turns singing all through the night. The herd was followed by the most important member of the team, a cook in a chuck wagon, who fed the crew three hot meals a day and also carried medicine. That responsibility was commonly given to an African American.

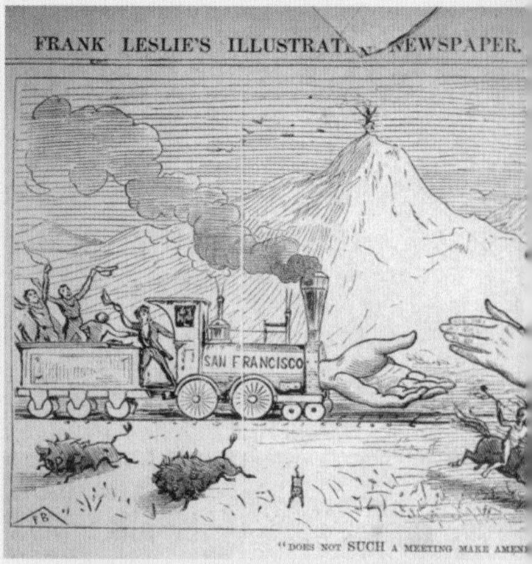

FRANK LESLIE'S ILLUSTRAT
NEWSPAPER.
SAN FRANCISCO
"DOES NOT SUCH A MEETING MAKE AMENI

Frank Leslie's Illustrated newspaper, May 29, 1869–LOC

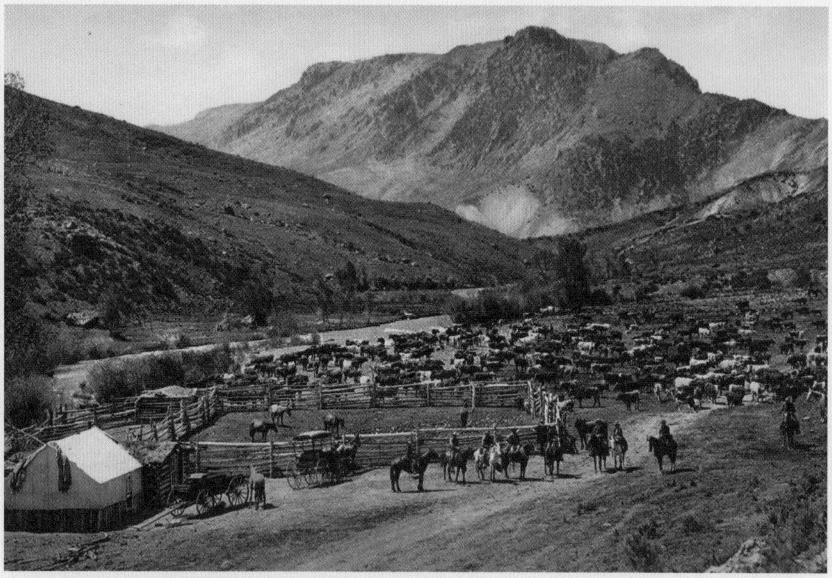

Colorado, "Round up" on the Cimarron, Detroit Photographic. c1898. LoC

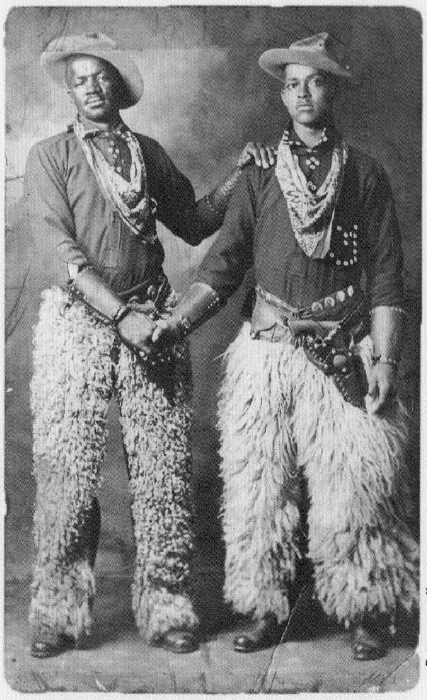

Private collection

Photographs were not available on a large scale until the 1900s, and photos of cowboys–especially of African American cowboys–are extremely rare. In the image above, the studio setting and the round corners indicate that it's probably a postcard from the early 1900s, but the photographer and the exact date are unknown.

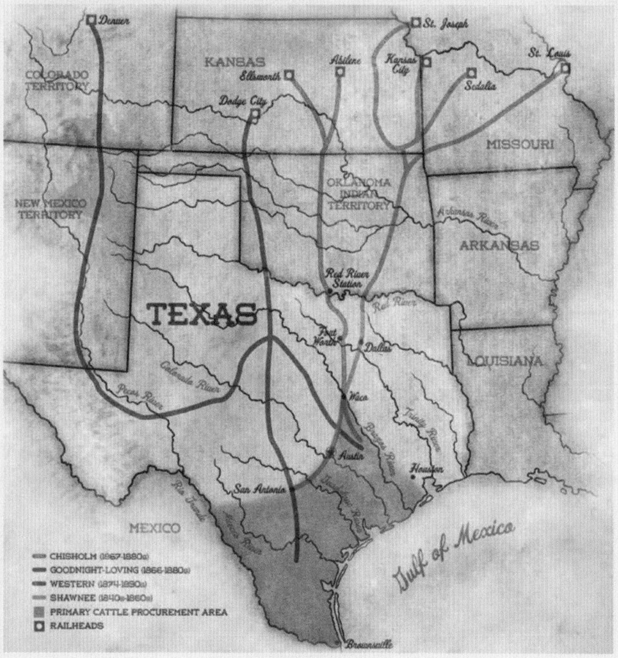

Denver
St. Joseph
KANSAS
Abilene
Kansas City
St. Louis
COLORADO TERRITORY
Ellsworth
Sedalia
Dodge City
MISSOURI
OKLAHOMA INDIAN TERRITORY
NEW MEXICO TERRITORY
Arkansas River
ARKANSAS
Red River Station
TEXAS
Red River
Fort Worth
Dallas
LOUISIANA
Colorado River
Pecos River
Waco
Austin
Houston
San Antonio
MEXICO
Gulf of Mexico
Brownsville
CHISHOLM (1867-1880s)
GOODNIGHT-LOVING (1866-1880s)
WESTERN (1874-1890s)
SHAWNEE (1840s-1860s)
PRIMARY CATTLE PROCUREMENT AREA
RAILHEADS

Exploring the Chisholm Trail, Texas Historical Commission

The cattle drives started around 1867 with the Chisholm Trail to Abilene, a newly created cattle-shipping depot. They lasted only until the 1890s, by which time the railroads had expanded.

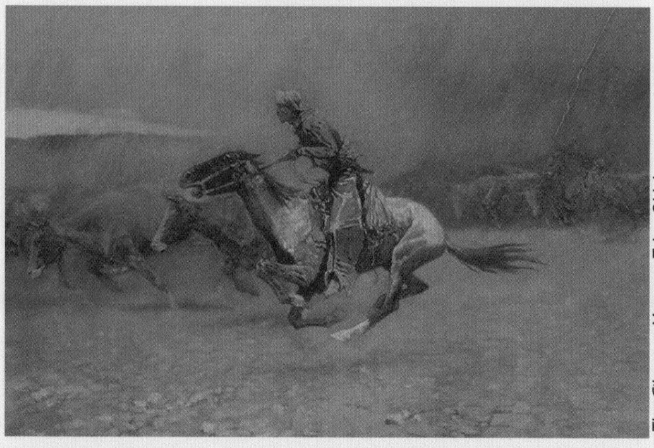

The Gilcrease Museum, Tulsa, Oklahoma

Much of the pictorial record of the life of a cowboy was provided by painters and artists, as in this 1908 painting by Frederic S. Remington, The Stampede.

[May 29, 1869.

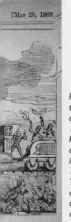

For much of the 1800s, the only way to travel through the West was on horseback or in a covered wagon. But on May 10, 1869, the Union Pacific and the Central Pacific Railroads were joined in Utah, creating the first transcontinental railroad in the United States. It stretched over 1900 miles and changed history forever. The railroad was built by between 15,000 and 20,000 Chinese immigrants, many of whom perished in the process. Their contribution deserves to be more fairly acknowledged.

BUFFALO SOLDIERS

The Civil War marked the first time that African Americans were allowed to serve in the US military. Following Emancipation, many former slaves joined the army and were deployed to frontier territories on the Great Plains to fight in what became known as the Indian Wars. As the United States expanded its borders, violent conflicts erupted between settlers, Native Americans, and Mexicans in the area. Among the soldiers sent to serve in the West were two infantry units (foot soldiers) and two cavalry units (horsemen) made up entirely of African Americans. These all-Black units were greatly respected for their bravery and skill in battle. Soon, they earned the name of "Buffalo Soldiers" among Plain Indians, a great honor as the buffalo was held in the highest esteem by the nomadic tribes such as the Blackfoot, Cheyenne, Comanche, Crow, Gros Ventre, Sioux, and the many others who depended on it. Other historians think that this name may have been given because African Americans' curly hair resembled that of buffaloes. Yet another reason might be that the poorly equipped soldiers used buffalo skins to protect themselves from subzero temperatures.

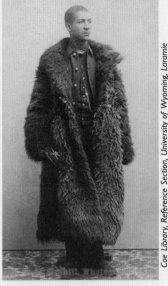

Coe Library, Reference Section, University of Wyoming, Laramie

25th Infantry soldier wearing a buffalo-hide coat, photographed by John C. H. Grabill in Sturgis, Dakota Territory, circa 1886.

BARBED WIRE AND THE END OF THE WILD WEST

As rail networks expanded across the country and methods for industrial refrigeration improved, the need for long cattle drives diminished. Barbed wire was another invention that shaped America in the late 1800s by changing the way ranches were operated. Before the widespread use of barbed wire, there was no effective way to fence in roaming cattle. Wooden fences were too expensive and not always reliable, and hedges used in other countries took too long to grow. This meant that ranchers had to hire as many skilled cowboys as they could to muster cattle. But barbed wire was cheap and durable: it withstood wind, rain, and snow and required almost no upkeep. Joseph Glidden (who found the inspiration in his wife's hairpins) was granted his first patent for it in 1874. By the 1890s, the Great Plains were all but fenced in. Indigenous peoples were forced off their land onto reservations, and the days of the open frontier were over.

J. F. GLIDDEN.
Wire-Fences.
No.157,124.
Patented Nov. 24, 1874.
Fig. I.
Fig. II.
Fig. III.
Witnesses:
Inventor:

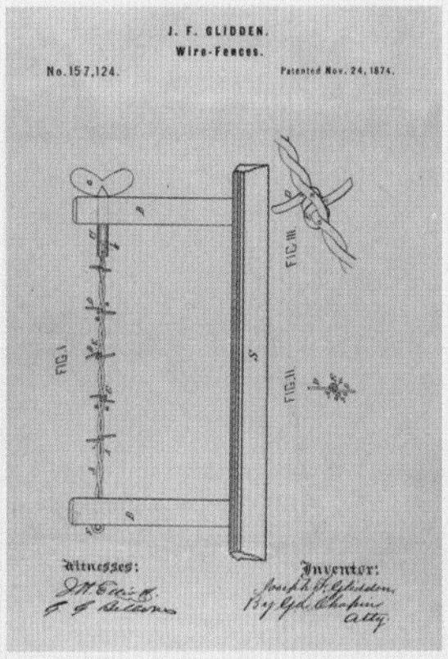

National Archives and Records Administration

Patent drawing for Joseph F. Glidden's improvement to barbed wire, Nov. 24, 1874

IF YOU WANT A FARM OR HOME
"THE BEST THING IN THE WEST"
IS THE
Atchison, Topeka & Santa Fe
RAILROAD
LANDS
IN SOUTHWEST KANSAS.
PRAIRIE
WOODLAND
A START ON THE PRAIRIE.
A START IN THE WOODS.
A.T.&S.F.R.R.
THE SAME PLACE AFTER SIX YEARS WORK AND PROFIT
THE SAME PLACE AFTER TEN YEARS WORK AND PROFIT
Temperate Climate, Excellent Health, Pure and Abundant Water.
GOOD SOIL FOR WHEAT, CORN AND FRUIT.
The Best Stock Country in the World.
For Full Information apply to
Or to
Agent,
LAND COMMISSIONER,
A. T. & S. F. R. R., Topeka, Kas.
Auskunft ertheilt, C. B. Schmidt, Deutscher Gen'l Agt., Topeka, Kan.

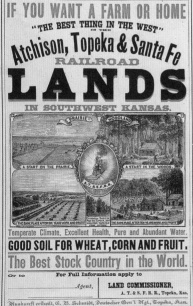

Courtesy: Kansas Historical Society, www.kshs.org

An Atchison, Topeka & Santa Fe Railroad poster advertising lands in southwest Kansas. The German language at the very bottom indicates the railroad's intent to appeal to European immigrants.

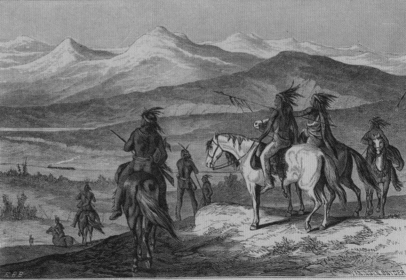

The Miriam and Ira D. Wallach Division of Art, Picture Collection, NYPL

"Indians viewing the Pacific Railroad," a wood engraving from 1871, shows Native Americans watching the progress of the "Iron Horse." After the 1862 Homestead Act and the Pacific Railway Act, they were forced to leave their ancestral homes.

NATIVE AMERICANS AND BLACK INDIANS

In the 1800s, much of the West was the loosely defined "Indian Territories," where many surviving Native Americans had been relocated. The indigenous peoples of the Great Plains, sometimes referred to as Plains Indians, had of course lived there since long before the arrival of the Europeans. Some Plains Indian tribes, like the Mandan and Hidatsa, engaged in sustainable agriculture, rotating maize (corn), beans, and squash. Most tribes though, such as the Crow and Lakota, led nomadic lives, hunting the millions of buffalo on the prairies. The horse had been introduced with the arrival of the Spaniards, and by the late 1700s, each member of tribes like the Apache and Comanche nations had at least one horse. Everything from hunting to warfare took place on horseback. Conflict and open war with US and European settlers had been a constant since their arrival, but in the late 1800s a calculated, all-out effort by the US government to exterminate the millions of buffalo on the plains had a devastating effect on the Plains Indians, as their main food source disappeared. Railway companies joined the call for extermination: wild herds often destroyed train tracks and caused accidents. Troops, rangers, and homesteaders conspired to chase Indigenous peoples off their lands and force them onto much smaller reservations. And as the West was divided up and fenced in, the territories became states (Arizona was the last in 1912).

African Americans and Native Americans share a long history in the West. There are many tales dating from the earliest Colonial times of runaway slaves being welcomed into Native American communities, and some tribes, like the Seminole nation, have numerous members with Black ancestry. Many African Americans, like Bass Reeves and Bob Lemmons, took refuge there and became fluent in the languages of local communities. They also learned horsemanship and wrangling skills from Native Americans, who were some of the finest cowboys.

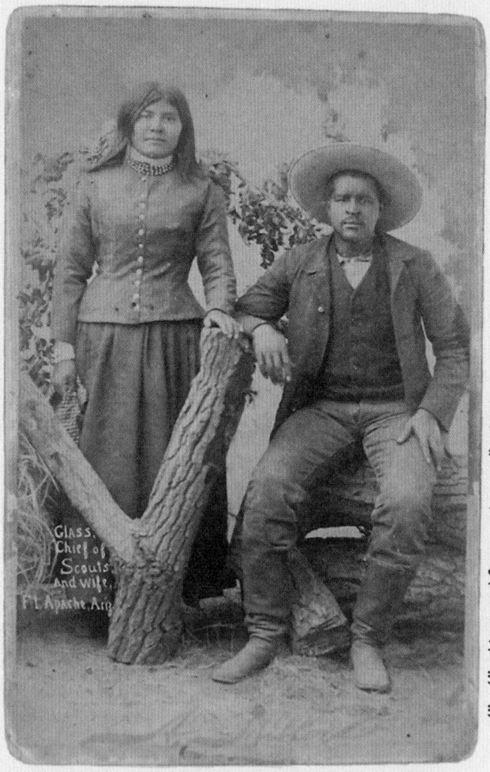
Glass,
Chief of
Scouts
and Wife,

4" x 6" cabinet card from a private collection

Very popular in the 19th century, cabinet cards were usually photographic portraits taken in a studio. This one shows John Glass, Chief of Scouts in the US Cavalry during the Apache Wars, and his wife, a member of the Apache nation. It was taken in the 1880s by Andrew Miller in the Arizona Territory.

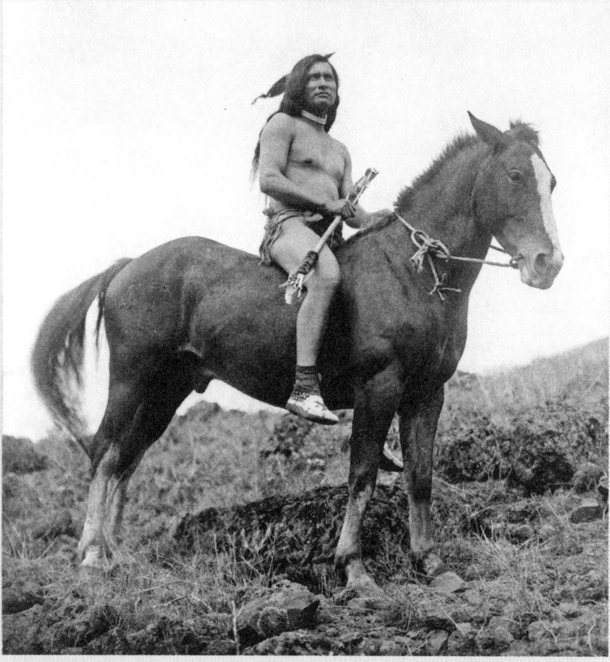

Library of Congress. Edward S. Curtis Collection. Curtis no. 2924-10.

"The Old Warrior," Nez Percé man on horseback, a 1910 print from Edward S. Curtis's 20-volume work, The North American Indian. *The ethnographer's massive work contributed to painting a romanticized picture of Native Americans at the same time as their survival and their culture were under threat and their lands were being appropriated.*

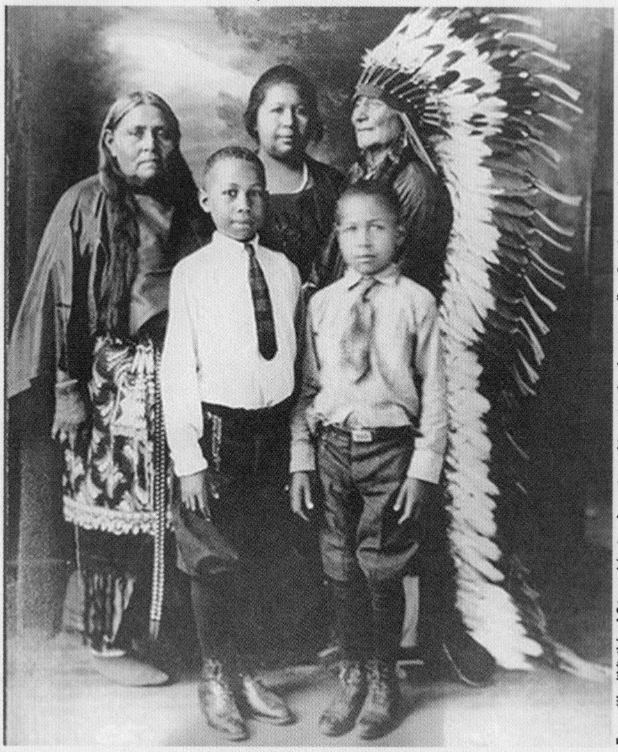

From "IndiVisible: African-Native American Lives in the Americas," a Smithsonian Institute traveling exhibit

Family from the Comanche Nation, Oklahoma, early 1900s. The elder woman, Ta-Tat-ty, and her husband, Ta-Ten-e-queris, frame their niece, Wife-per (center), also known as Frances E. Wright. Frances's father was a Buffalo Soldier who deserted and married into the Comanches. Henry (center left) and Lorenzano (center right) are the sons of Frances, who married an African American man.

AFRICAN AMERICANS ON THE FRONTIER

While it is estimated that as many as a third of cowboys riding the trails in Texas were black, the number of African American cowboys in other frontier states like Montana or Oregon was much smaller. Even as late as the 1890s, there were barely a thousand African Americans living in Oregon, where racism was particularly strong. This doesn't mean that they didn't play an important part in the history of those places. John Ware *(pictured at right with his family)* was a famous horseman who brought the first cattle from Texas into southern Alberta, Canada, in 1882. The well-known fur trader James P. Beckwourth *(far right)* was a gambler, explorer, and entrepreneur who roamed the mountains and plains of the Territories.

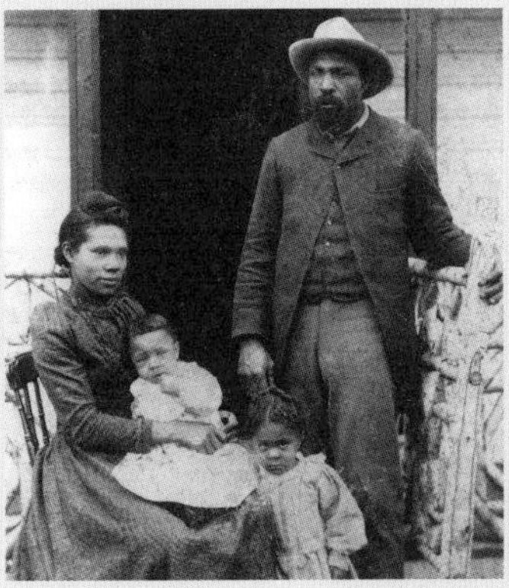

John Ware and his family in 1896. Glenbow Archives

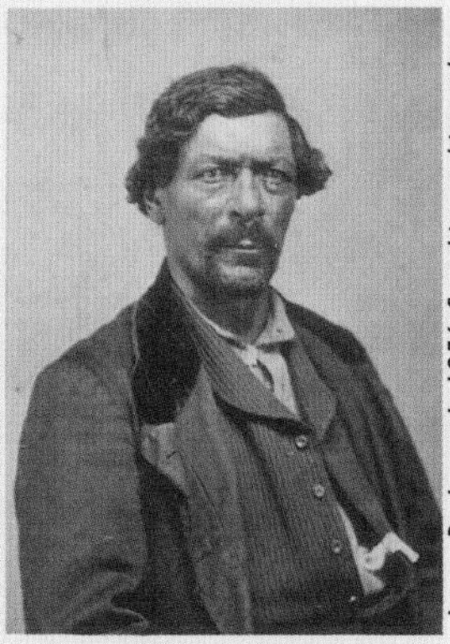

James Beckwourth, 1856, from his autobiography

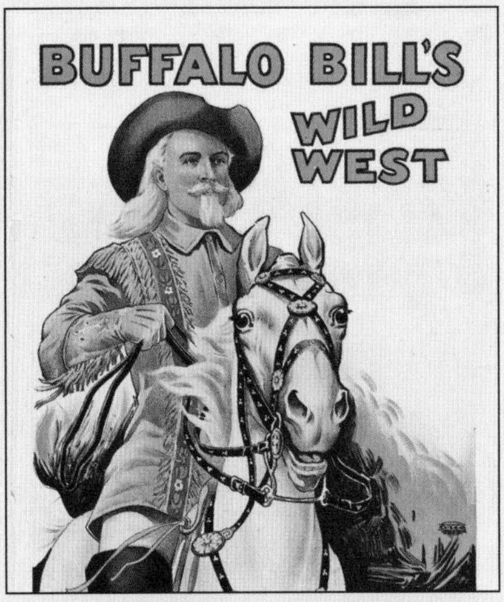
BUFFALO BILL'S
WILD
WEST

Buffalo Bill's Wild West Sells Floto Circus, 1926 Circus Poster

MYTHMAKING AND THE WILD WEST

By the 1890s, cowboys had been fenced in by barbed wire, and the days of the cattle drives were over. This was when the myths of the Wild West became wildly popular through rodeos and stage shows like Buffalo Bill's Wild West. As the role of cowboys shifted from ranch hand to entertainer, new opportunities arose for African Americans to showcase their skills in horse racing, bucking, bull riding, and wrangling. Some African American rodeo performers, such as Bill Pickett and Jesse Stahl, became quite famous. But the Buffalo Bill stage shows, which toured the US, England, and Europe, didn't feature African Americans or Hispanics. Native Americans were well represented, but only as villains or savages who were inevitably defeated by white cowboys. In this way, a mythology of the Wild West that ignores true history was created and repeated in films, TV shows, and novels even to this day.

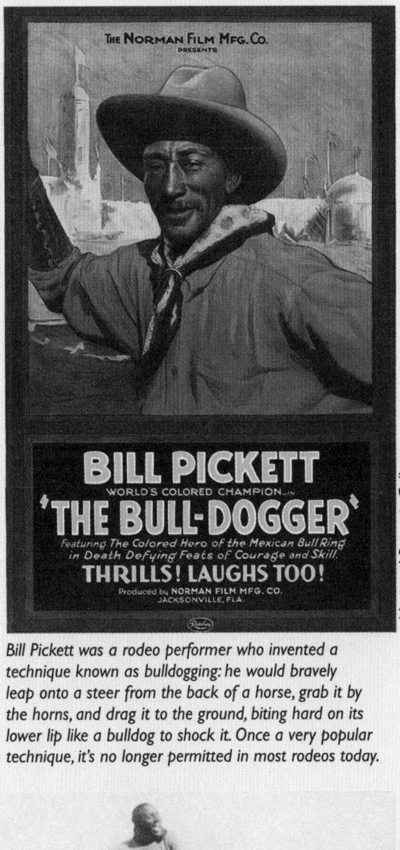
THE NORMAN FILM MFG. CO.
PRESENTS
BILL PICKETT
WORLD'S COLORED CHAMPION IN
'THE BULL-DOGGER'
Featuring The Colored Hero of the Mexican Bull Ring in Death Defying Feats of Courage and Skill.
THRILLS! LAUGHS TOO!
Produced by NORMAN FILM MFG. CO.
JACKSONVILLE, FLA.

National Portrait Gallery

Bill Pickett was a rodeo performer who invented a technique known as bulldogging: he would bravely leap onto a steer from the back of a horse, grab it by the horns, and drag it to the ground, biting hard on its lower lip like a bulldog to shock it. Once a very popular technique, it's no longer permitted in most rodeos today.

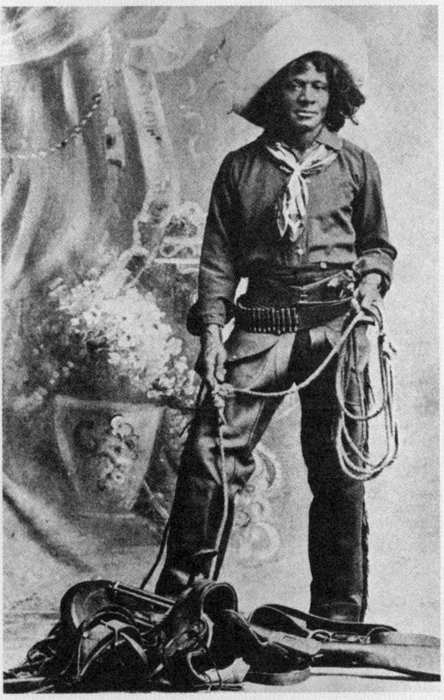

From Nat Love's self-published autobiography, Kansas Historical Society

Nat Love became the emblematic African American cowboy when he wrote his autobiography in 1907. Pictured here circa 1900, Nat was born into slavery but taught himself how to read and write. He worked as a cowboy in Dodge City, Kansas, where he fought cattle rustlers and drank with Billy the Kid. Nat Love was also known as "Deadwood Dick" for outshooting and outwrangling every other cowboy at the July 4th celebrations in Deadwood, South Dakota, in 1876.

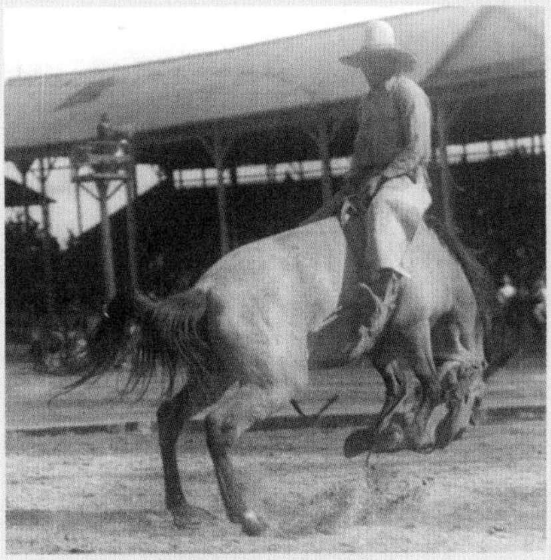

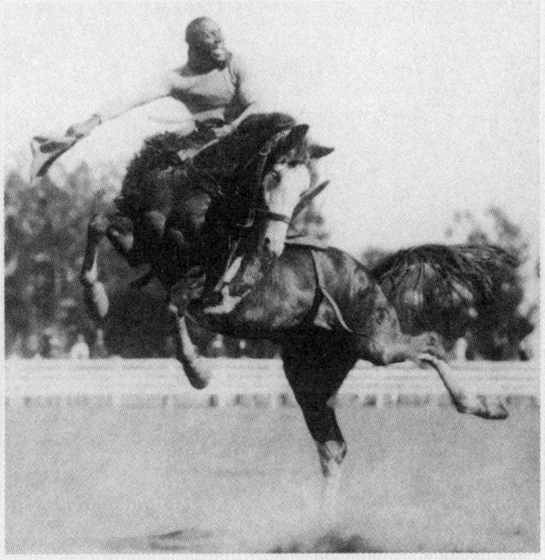

Oregon Historical Society Research Library

Jesse Stahl (1879-1935) riding backwards on a horse named Gravedigger (above left). Stahl was known as a top-notch horseman and a first-class gentleman. Stahl and another black cowboy, Ty Stokes, rode a bucking horse seated back to back in was what was called a "suicide ride." Stahl was inducted into the Cowboy Hall of Fame in Oklahoma City in 1979.

IS THE LONE RANGER BASED ON BASS REEVES?

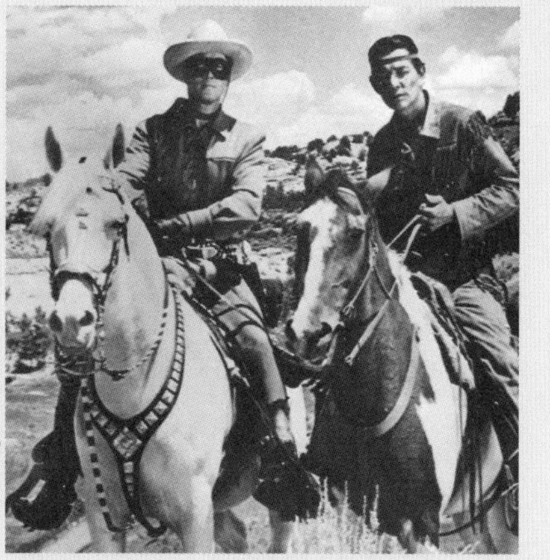

Lone Ranger and Tonto 1956, ABC Television

Bass Reeves *(right)* was a legend in his own time. Born into slavery in Arkansas in 1838, Bass Reeves grew up in Texas, and when his owner joined the Confederate Army during the Civil War, Reeves was taken along too. He managed to escape and fled to the Indian Territories in the West. Until the Emancipation Proclamation in 1863, he lived there among the Cherokee, Creek, and Seminole nations, where he was welcomed as a fugitive slave and learned to speak their languages. Reeves's reputation for fairness and his ability to speak Native American languages meant he was recruited as a Deputy US Marshal—the first black marshal west of the Mississippi River. Reeves brought over 3000 fugitives to justice, without ever being gravely wounded. He often worked alongside Native Americans and relied on his wits to outsmart outlaws on the run. Bass Reeves was so committed to serving justice that once, he even arrested his own son and brought him in for trial. If Bass Reeves's story seems familiar to you, it might be because he shares many of his amazing traits with a character known as the Lone Ranger *(above left)*, the subject of a long-running television show and several movies. One thing is different, though: the Lone Ranger has always been depicted as a white man. In fact, most books and movies set in the Old West focus on white characters and leave out the essential roles played by African Americans.

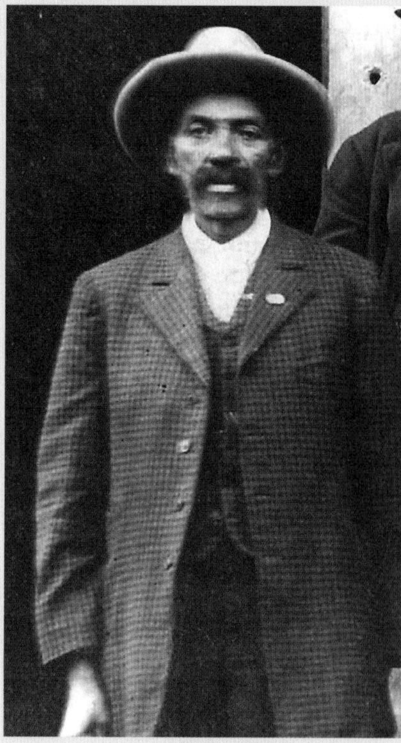

Oklahoma Historical Society

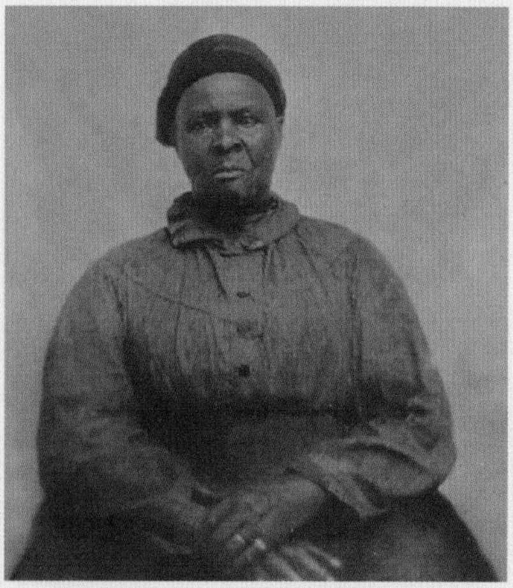

Ursuline Sisters Archive, Great Falls, Montana

BLACK WOMEN PIONEERS

Life wasn't easy on the frontier for black cowboys, but it was even more difficult for African American women. Like Mary Fields *(left)*, many women who had been born into slavery and then freed worked as laundresses, domestic servants, and cooks. It was also common for black women to work as teachers and midwives.

Other remarkable women of the era include Elizabeth Thorn Scott Flood, who fought for the right of black children to receive an education, and Mary Ellen Pleasant *(right)*, an entrepreneur who made a fortune in San Francisco during the Gold Rush and fought a series of legal battles to protect the civil rights of African Americans.

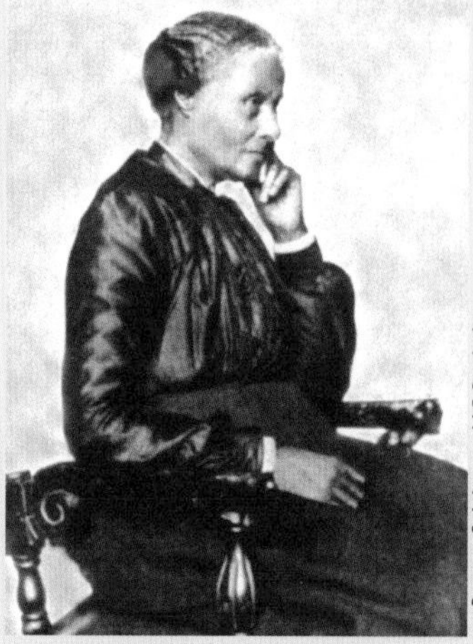

Bancroft Library, UC Berkeley

BOB LEMMONS AND BLACK HOMESTEADERS

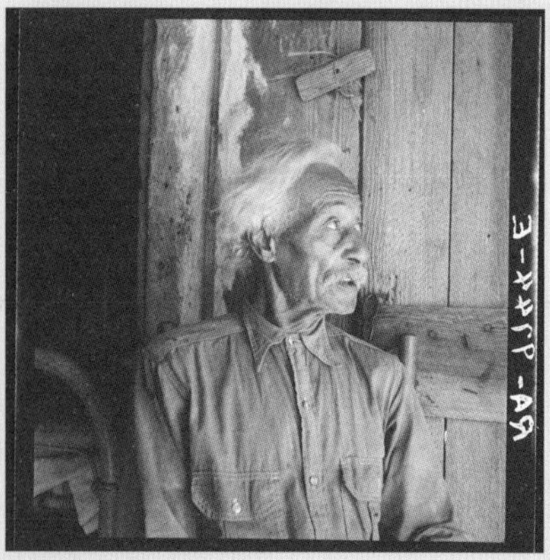

Nitrate negative, see page 37, LOCN 2017763146

Photographer Dorothea Lange (1895-1965) interviewed Bob Lemmons in 1936 as part of her work for the WPA Slave Narratives project, a government-funded project during the Great Depression.

Some black pioneers like Bob Lemmons lived through the cowboy era and made enough money to settle on their own ranches. Bob Lemmons married Barbarita Rosales in 1881, and the couple had eight children. They faced discrimination because Bob was African American and Barbarita was Chicana ("mixed" marriages were illegal). Despite this, Bob helped his neighbors through the difficult times of the Great Depression and lived to be 99 years old.

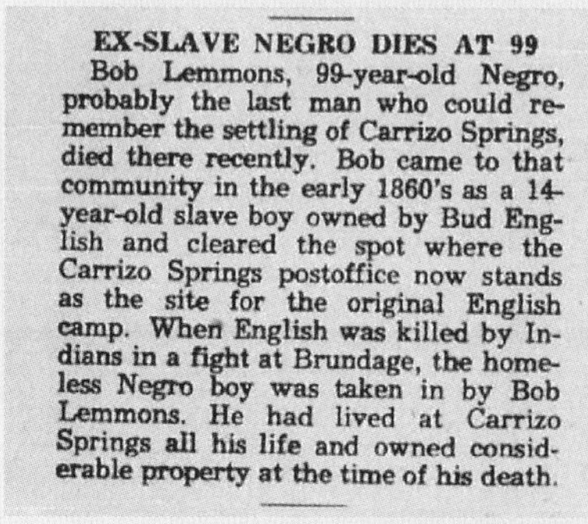

EX-SLAVE NEGRO DIES AT 99

Bob Lemmons, 99-year-old Negro, probably the last man who could remember the settling of Carrizo Springs, died there recently. Bob came to that community in the early 1860's as a 14-year-old slave boy owned by Bud English and cleared the spot where the Carrizo Springs postoffice now stands as the site for the original English camp. When English was killed by Indians in a fight at Brundage, the homeless Negro boy was taken in by Bob Lemmons. He had lived at Carrizo Springs all his life and owned considerable property at the time of his death.

The Cameron Herald, February 12, 1948

The obituary for Bob Lemmons in the local newspaper covering Carrizo Springs, Dimmit County, Texas.

TIMELINE

MARY FIELDS *born 1832?, Hickman County, Tennessee — died December 5, 1914, Cascade, Montana*

BASS REEVES *born 1838, Crawford County, Arkansas — died January 12, 1910, Muskogee, Oklahoma*

BOB LEMMONS *born 1848, Lockport, Texas — died December 23, 1947, Carrizo Springs, Texas*

1609–1924: *American Indian Wars (considered to have ended in 1924 with the conclusion of the Apache Wars)*

1803: *USA completes Louisiana Purchase, more than doubling the size of its territory*

1810: *Mexico declares independence from Spain (not conceded by Spain until 1821)*

1830: *Andrew Jackson signs Indian Removal Act, paving the way for the forced removal of Native American nations and the creation of reservations*

1836: *On May 2, Texas declares independence from Mexico*

1844: *Texas annexed by the USA on June 23, 1844*

1846-1848: *Mexican-American War (Mexico cedes the rest of the Southwest to the USA)*

1861–1865: *Civil War*   **1863:** *The Emancipation Proclamation frees more than 3 million slaves*

1800	1810	1820	1830	1840	1850	1860	1870	1880	1890	1900	1910	1920	1930	1940	1950

1862: *Thanks to the Homestead Act, settlers who claim & occupy a minimum of 160 acres of land in the West can claim ownership after five years.*

1866: *Five regiments of African American soldiers are formed to fight in the Indian Wars, becoming known as Buffalo Soldiers. Era of the great Texas cattle drives begins.*

1869: *The Central Pacific Railroad and the Union Pacific Railroad combine into the First Transcontinental Railroad.*

1873: *On July 21, Jesse James and his gang complete their first train robbery.*

1885-87: *Two harsh winters followed by two dry summers kill 80 to 90 percent of the cattle on the Plains.*

1890: *11th US Census reveals that the spread of the population means there is no longer a "frontier."*

1912: *Arizona becomes the last state admitted to the Union in the Old West era.*

1916: *Last ever stagecoach robbery in US history takes place in Nevada. Bandits are swiftly brought to justice after attacking a US Postal Service stagecoach.*

Cowboys in the Badlands, by Thomas Eakins, 1888 painting

THE WILD WEST: Key dates and defining moments

FURTHER READING & RESOURCES

History is complex and fascinating. You can broaden your understanding of factual information when you shift your point of view. Research resources are vast, but here's a short list of books and other resources you might enjoy:

BLACK COWBOY, WILD HORSES, by Julius Lester and Jerry Pinkney. Dial Books, 1998. *An illustrated tale of Bob Lemmons and his incredible horsemanship. Ages 4-8.*

HEART AND SOUL: THE STORY OF AMERICA AND AFRICAN AMERICANS, by Kadir Nelson. Balzer + Bray, 2011. *An illustrated story of hope and inspiration covering the history of African Americans. Ages 6-10*

BAD NEWS FOR OUTLAWS: THE REMARKABLE LIFE OF BASS REEVES, DEPUTY U.S. MARSHAL, by Vaunda Micheaux Nelson (Author), R. Gregory Christie (Illustrator). Carolrhoda Books, 2009. *Winner of the 2010 Coretta Scott King Author Award. Ages 6-8*

THE LEGEND OF BASS REEVES, by Gary Paulsen. Laurel Leaf, 2008. *A fictionalized narrative based on the life of Bass Reeves. Ages 10+*

BLACK COWBOYS OF THE OLD WEST: TRUE, SENSATIONAL, AND LITTLE-KNOWN STORIES FROM HISTORY, by Tricia Martineau Wagner. TwoDot, 2010. *Ten biographies of black cowboys in a jaunty and readable style. Ages 12+*

AFRICAN AMERICAN WOMEN OF THE OLD WEST, by Tricia Martineau Wagner. TwoDot, 2007. *Little-known African American women from the frontier. Ages 12+*

BLACK FRONTIERS: A HISTORY OF AFRICAN AMERICAN HEROES IN THE OLD WEST, by Lillian Schlissel. Aladdin,

2000. *An informative overview of the lives of African Americans in the Old West. Ages 12+*

BLACK GUN, SILVER STAR: THE LIFE AND LEGEND OF FRONTIER MARSHAL BASS REEVES, by Art T. Burton. UNP - Bison Books, 2008. *Reproduces many of the primary sources. 12+*

Other Resources:

The Library of Congress, the National Archives, and libraries such as the New York Public Library provide access to documents from the past. Many states, museums, and historical associations also offer a wealth of information on local history. For example:

WWW.KANSASMEMORY.ORG/ *Primary sources from the Kansas Historical Society*

HTTPS://TSHAONLINE.ORG/HANDBOOK/ONLINE/ARTICLES/ARBO1 *from the Texas State Historical Association*

Black American West Museum, in Denver, CO, HTTPS://BAWMHC.ORG/

The Buffalo Soldier Museum, in Houston, TX, HTTP://BUFFALOSOLDIERMUSEUM.COM/

National Multicultural Western Heritage Museum, in Fort Worth, TX, HTTP://WWW.COWBOYSOFCOLOR.ORG/

Smithsonian National Museum of African American History & Culture, in Washington, DC, HTTPS://NMAAHC.SI.EDU/

COMICS: EASY AS ABC!
by Ivan Brunetti

FOR VISUAL READERS
TOON BOOKS®

TOON Graphics are comics and visual narratives that bring the text to life in a way that captures young readers' imaginations. When the authors are also artists, they can convey their creative vision with pictures as well as words. They can enhance the overarching theme and present important details visually along with the text. Reluctant and seasoned readers alike will sharpen both their literal and inferential reading skills. The award-winning collection covers many middle-grade curriculum themes such as Comparative Literature, Folktales, Greek Mythology, Diversity and Multiculturalism, Coming of Age, and Transportation, among many others. Deriving meaning from reading with the aid of visuals may be the best way to become a lifelong reader, one who knows how to read for pleasure and for information—a reader who loves to read.

LOST IN NYC: A SUBWAY ADVENTURE
by Nadja Spiegelman
& Sergio García Sánchez

THE DRAGON SLAYER: FOLKTALES
FROM LATIN AMERICA
by Jaime Hernandez

THE WHITE SNAKE, based on a fairy
tale by the Grimm Brothers
by Ben Nadler

THE SECRET OF
THE STONE FROG
by David Nytra

THESEUS and The Minotaur / ORPHEUS in The Underworld / OEDIPUS, Trapped By Destiny
by Yvan Pommaux

CAST AWAY ON THE LETTER A / THE WILD PIANO / THE SUSPENDED CASTLE
by Fred

HANSEL & GRETEL
by Neil Gaiman & Lorenzo Mattotti

WWW.TOON-BOOKS.COM